PENGUIN BOOKS — GREAT FOOD

The Campaign for Domestic Happiness

ISABELLA BEETON was born in London in 1836, one of twenty-one brothers and sisters. Between 1859 and 1861 Beeton wrote articles on cooking and household management for her husband's publications. The collection of these articles became the single-volume *Book of Household Management*, a guide to all aspects of running a household in Victorian Britain that included not only recipes, home-made remedies and how to deal with servants' pay but also smaller yet surprising subjects such as violence, cruelty and death. It remains a classic piece of domestic literature, providing us with invaluable insight into the Victorian household. Beeton died just four years after its publication, at the age of twenty-eight.

The Campaign for Domestic Happiness

ISABELLA BEETON

PENGUIN BOOKS

PENGUIN BOOKS

Published by the Penguin Group
Penguin Group (USA) Inc., 375 Hudson Street, New York, New York 10014, U.S.A.
Penguin Group (Canada), 90 Eglinton Avenue East, Suite 700, Toronto, Ontario, Canada M4P 2Y3 (a division of Pearson Penguin Canada Inc.)
Penguin Books Ltd, 80 Strand, London WC2R 0RL, England
Penguin Ireland, 25 St. Stephen's Green, Dublin 2, Ireland (a division of Penguin Books Ltd)
Penguin Books Australia Ltd, 250 Camberwell Road, Camberwell, Victoria 3124, Australia (a division of Pearson Australia Group Pty Ltd)
Penguin Books India Pvt Ltd, 11 Community Centre, Panchsheel Park, New Delhi – 110 017, India
Penguin Group (NZ), 67 Apollo Drive, Rosedale, Auckland 0632, New Zealand (a division of Pearson New Zealand Ltd)
Penguin Books (South Africa) (Pty) Ltd, 24 Sturdee Avenue, Rosebank, Johannesburg 2196, South Africa

Penguin Books Ltd, Registered Offices: 80 Strand, London WC2R 0RL, England

The Book of Household Management first published 1861
This extract first published in Great Britain in Penguin Books 2011
First published in the USA by Viking Studio, a member of Penguin Group (USA) Inc. 2011
1 3 5 7 9 10 8 6 4 2

Set in 10.75/13 pt Berkeley Oldstyle Book
Typeset by Jouve (UK), Milton Keynes
Printed in Great Britain by Clays Ltd, St Ives plc

Cover design based on a pattern from a plate by Spode Ceramic Works, *c.* 1830. Bone china painted with enamels and gilded. (Photograph copyright © Victoria & Albert Museum.) Picture research by Samantha Johnson. Lettering by Stephen Raw.

ISBN: 978–0–241–95634–2

www.penguin.com

Penguin Books is committed to a sustainable future for our business, our readers and our planet. This book is made from paper certified by the Forest Stewardship Council.

Contents

Preface vii

The Mistress 1

Recipes for Soup 33

Recipes for Fish 37

Recipes for Sauces, Pickles and Gravies 43

Recipes for Beef 50

Recipes for Mutton and Lamb 54

Recipes for Pork 58

Recipes for Veal 62

Recipes for Poultry and Rabbits 64

Recipes for Game 71

Recipes for Vegetables 75

Recipes for Puddings and Pastry 79

Recipes for Creams and Sweet Dishes 82

Recipes for Confectionary, Ices and Dessert Dishes 86

Recipes for Milk, Butter, Cheese and Eggs 92

Recipes for Cakes 97

Recipes for Beverages 100
Recipes for Invalid Cookery 106

Preface

I must frankly own, that if I had known, beforehand, that this book would have cost me the labour which it has, I should never have been courageous enough to commence it. What moved me, in the first instance, to attempt a work like this, was the discomfort and suffering which I had seen brought upon men and women by household mismanagement. I have always thought that there is no more fruitful source of family discontent than a housewife's badly-cooked dinners and untidy ways. Men are now so well served out of doors – at their clubs, well-ordered taverns, and dining-houses, that in order to compete with the attractions of these places, a mistress must be thoroughly acquainted with the theory and practice of cookery, as well as be perfectly conversant with all the other arts of making and keeping a comfortable home.

In this book I have attempted to give, under the chapters devoted to cookery, an intelligible arrangement to every recipe, a list of the ingredients, a plain statement of the mode of preparing each dish, and a careful estimate of its cost, the number of people for whom it is sufficient, and the time when it is seasonable. For the matter of the recipes, I am indebted, in some measure, to many correspondents of the *Englishwoman's Domestic Magazine*, who have obligingly placed at my disposal their formulas for many original preparations. A large private circle has also rendered me considerable service. A diligent study of the works of the best modern writers on cookery was also necessary to the faithful fulfilment of my task. Friends in England, Scotland, Ireland, France, and Germany, have also very materially aided me [. . .] In the department belonging to the Cook I have striven, too, to make my work something more than a Cookery Book, and have, therefore, on the best authority that I could obtain, given an account of the natural history of the animals and vegetables which we use as food [. . .]

I wish here to acknowledge the kind letters and congratulations I have received during the progress of this work, and have only further to add that I trust the result of the four years' incessant labour which I have expended will not be altogether unacceptable to some of my countrymen and countrywomen.

ISABELLA BEETON

The Mistress

> Strength and honour are her clothing; and she shall rejoice in time to come. She openeth her mouth with wisdom; and in her tongue is the law of kindness. She looketh well to the ways of her household; and eateth not the bread of idleness. Her children arise up, and call her blessed; her husband also, and he praiseth her. – PROVERBS 31:25–28

As with the commander of an army, or the leader of any enterprise, so is it with the mistress of a house. Her spirit will be seen through the whole establishment; and just in proportion as she performs her duties intelligently and thoroughly, so will her domestics follow in her path. Of all those acquirements, which more particularly belong to the feminine character, there are none which take a higher rank, in our estimation, than such as enter into a knowledge of household duties; for on these are perpetually dependent the happiness, comfort, and well-being of a family. In this opinion we are borne out by the author of *The Vicar of Wakefield*, who says: 'The modest virgin, the prudent wife, and the careful matron, are much more serviceable in life than petticoated philosophers, blustering heroines, or virago queens. She who makes her husband and her children happy, who reclaims the one from vice and trains up the other to virtue, is a much greater character than ladies described in romances, whose whole occupation is to murder mankind with shafts from their quiver, or their eyes.'

Pursuing this picture, we may add, that to be a good housewife does not necessarily imply an abandonment of proper pleasures or amusing recreation; and we think it the more necessary to express this, as the performance of the duties of a mistress may, to some minds, perhaps seem to be incompatible with the enjoyment of life. Let us, however, now proceed to describe some of those home qualities and virtues which are necessary to the proper management of a Household, and then point out the plan which may be the most profitably pursued for the daily regulation of its affairs.

Early rising is one of the most essential qualities which enter into good Household Management, as it is not only the parent of health, but of innumerable other advantages. Indeed, when a mistress is an early riser, it is almost certain that her house will be orderly and well-managed. On the contrary, if she remain in bed till a late hour, then the domestics, who, as we have before observed, invariably partake somewhat of their mistress's character, will surely become sluggards. To self-indulgence all are more or less disposed, and it is not to be expected that servants are freer from this fault than the heads of houses. The great Lord Chatham thus gave his advice in reference to this subject: 'I would have inscribed on the curtains of your bed, and the walls of your chamber, "If you do not rise early, you can make progress in nothing."'

Cleanliness is also indispensable to health, and must be studied both in regard to the person and the house, and all that it contains. Cold or tepid baths should be employed every morning, unless, on account of illness or other circumstances, they should be deemed objectionable.

Frugality and economy are home virtues, without which no household can prosper. Dr Johnson says: 'Frugality may be termed the daughter of Prudence, the sister of Temperance, and the parent of Liberty. He that is extravagant will quickly become poor, and poverty will enforce dependence and invite corruption.' The necessity of practising economy should be evident to every one, whether in the possession of an income no more than sufficient for a family's requirements, or of a large fortune, which puts financial adversity out of the question. We must always remember that it is a great merit in housekeeping to manage a little well. 'He is a good waggoner,' says Bishop Hall, 'that can turn in a little room. To live well in abundance is the praise of the estate, not of the person. I will study more how to give a good account of my little, than how to make it more.' In this there is true wisdom, and it may be added, that those who can manage a little well, are most likely to succeed in their management of larger matters. Economy and frugality must never, however, be allowed to degenerate into parsimony and meanness.

[. . .]

Friendships should not be hastily formed, nor the heart given, at once, to every new-comer. There are ladies who uniformly smile at, and approve everything and everybody, and who possess neither the courage to reprehend vice, nor the generous warmth to defend virtue. The friendship of such persons is without attachment, and their love without affection or even preference.

They imagine that every one who has any penetration is ill-natured, and look coldly on a discriminating judgment. It should be remembered, however, that this discernment does not always proceed from an uncharitable temper, but that those who possess a long experience and thorough knowledge of the world, scrutinize the conduct and dispositions of people before they trust themselves to the first fair appearances. Addison, who was not deficient in a knowledge of mankind, observes that 'a friendship, which makes the least noise, is very often the most useful; for which reason, I should prefer a prudent friend to a zealous one'. And Joanna Baillie tells us that:

> Friendship is no plant of hasty growth,
> Though planted in esteem's deep-fixed soil,
> The gradual culture of kind intercourse
> Must bring it to perfection.

Hospitality is a most excellent virtue; but care must be taken that the love of company, for its own sake, does not become a prevailing passion; for then the habit is no longer hospitality, but dissipation. Reality and truthfulness in this, as in all other duties of life, are the points to be studied; for, as Washington Irving well says, 'There is an emanation from the heart in genuine hospitality, which cannot be described, but is immediately felt, and puts the stranger at once at his ease.' With respect to the continuance of friendships, however, it may be found necessary, in some cases, for a mistress to relinquish, on assuming the responsibility of a household, many of those commenced in the earlier part of her life. This will be the more requisite, if the number still retained be quite equal to her means and opportunities.

In conversation, trifling occurrences, such as small disappointments, petty annoyances, and other every-day incidents, should never be mentioned to your friends. The extreme injudiciousness of repeating these will be at once apparent, when we reflect on the unsatisfactory discussions which they too frequently occasion, and on the load of advice which they are the cause of being tendered, and which is, too often, of a kind neither to be useful nor agreeable. Greater events, whether of joy or sorrow, should be communicated to friends; and, on such occasions, their sympathy gratifies and comforts. If the mistress be a wife, never let an account of her husband's failings pass her lips; and in cultivating the power of conversation, she should keep the versified advice of Cowper continually in her memory, that it

> Should flow like water after summer showers,
> Not as if raised by mere mechanic powers.

In reference to its style, Dr Johnson, who was himself greatly distinguished for his colloquial abilities, says that 'no style is more extensively acceptable than the narrative, because this does not carry an air of superiority over the rest of the company; and, therefore, is most likely to please them. For this purpose we should store our memory with short anecdotes and entertaining pieces of history. Almost every one listens with eagerness to extemporary history. Vanity often co-operates with curiosity; for he that is a hearer in one place wishes to qualify himself to be a principal speaker in some inferior company; and therefore more attention is given to narrations than anything else in conversation. It is true, indeed, that sallies of wit and quick replies are very pleasing in conversation; but they frequently tend to raise envy in some of the company: but the narrative way neither raises this, nor any other evil passion, but keeps all the company nearly upon an equality, and, if judiciously managed, will at once entertain and improve them all.'

Good temper should be cultivated by every mistress, as upon it the welfare of the household may be said to turn; indeed, its influence can hardly be overestimated, as it has the effect of moulding the characters of those around her, and of acting most beneficially on the happiness of the domestic circle. Every head of a household should strive to be cheerful, and should never fail to show a deep interest in all that appertains to the well-being of those who claim the protection of her roof. Gentleness, not partial and temporary, but universal and regular, should pervade her conduct; for where such a spirit is habitually manifested, it not only delights her children, but makes her domestics attentive and respectful; her visitors are also pleased by it, and their happiness is increased.

On the important subject of dress and fashion we cannot do better than quote an opinion from the eighth volume of the *Englishwoman's Domestic Magazine*. The writer there says, 'Let people write, talk, lecture, satirize, as they may, it cannot be denied that, whatever is the prevailing mode in attire, let it intrinsically be ever so absurd, it will never look as ridiculous as another, or as any other, which, however convenient, comfortable, or even becoming, is totally opposite in style to that generally worn.'

On purchasing articles of wearing apparel, whether it be a silk dress, a bonnet, shawl, or riband, it is well for the buyer to consider three things: 1. That it be not too expensive for her purse. 2. That its colour harmonize with her complexion, and its size and pattern with her figure. 3. That its tint allow of its being worn with the other garments she possesses. The quaint Fuller observes, that the good wife is none of our dainty dames, who love to appear in a variety of suits every day new, as if a gown, like a stratagem in war, were to be used but once. But our good wife sets up a sail according to the keel of her husband's estate; and, if of high parentage, she doth not so remember what she was by birth, that she forgets what she is by match.

To Brunettes, or those ladies having dark complexions, silks of a grave hue are adapted. For Blondes, or those having fair complexions, lighter colours are preferable, as the richer, deeper hues are too overpowering for the latter. The colours which go best together are green with violet; gold-colour with dark crimson or lilac; pale blue with scarlet; pink with black or white; and gray with scarlet or pink. A cold colour generally requires a warm tint to give life to it. Gray and pale blue, for instance, do not combine well, both being cold colours.

The dress of the mistress should always be adapted to her circumstances, and be varied with different occasions. Thus, at breakfast she should be attired in a very neat and simple manner, wearing no ornaments. If this dress should decidedly pertain only to the breakfast-hour, and be specially suited for such domestic occupations as usually follow that meal, then it would be well to exchange it before the time for receiving visitors, if the mistress be in the habit of doing so. It is still to be remembered, however, that, in changing the dress, jewellery and ornaments are not to be worn until the full dress for dinner is assumed.

The advice of Polonius to his son Laertes, in Shakespeare's tragedy of *Hamlet*, is most excellent; and although given to one of the male sex, will equally apply to a 'fayre ladye':

> Costly thy habit as thy purse can buy,
> But not express'd in fancy; rich, not gaudy;
> For the apparel oft proclaims the man.

Charity and benevolence are duties which a mistress owes to herself as well as to her fellow-creatures; and there is scarcely any income so small, but something may be spared from it, even if it be but 'the widow's mite'. It is to be always remembered, however, that it is the spirit of charity which imparts to the gift a value far beyond its actual amount, and is by far its better part.

> True Charity, a plant divinely nursed,
> Fed by the love from which it rose at first,
> Thrives against hope, and, in the rudest scene,
> Storms but enliven its unfading green;
> Exub'rant is the shadow it supplies,
> Its fruit on earth, its growth above the skies.

Visiting the houses of the poor is the only practical way really to understand the actual state of each family; and although there may be difficulties in following out this plan in the metropolis and other large cities, yet in country towns and rural districts these objections do not obtain. Great advantages may result from visits paid to the poor; for there being, unfortunately, much ignorance, generally, amongst them with respect to all household knowledge, there will be opportunities for advising and instructing them, in a pleasant and unobtrusive manner, in cleanliness, industry, cookery, and good management.

In marketing, that the best articles are the cheapest, may be laid down as a rule; and it is desirable, unless an experienced and confidential housekeeper be kept, that the mistress should herself purchase all provisions and stores needed for the house. If the mistress be a young wife, and not accustomed to order 'things for the house,' a little practice and experience will soon teach her who are the best tradespeople to deal with, and what are the best provisions to buy.

A housekeeping account-book should invariably be kept, and kept punctually and precisely. The plan for keeping household accounts, which we should recommend, would be to make an entry, that is, write down into a daily diary every amount paid on that particular day, be it ever so small; then, at the end of the month, let these various payments be ranged under their specific heads of Butcher, Baker, etc.; and thus will be seen the proportions paid to each tradesman, and any one month's expenses may be contrasted with another.

The housekeeping accounts should be balanced not less than once a month; so that you may see that the money you have in hand tallies with your account of it in your diary. Judge Haliburton never wrote truer words than when he said, 'No man is rich whose expenditure exceeds his means, and no one is poor whose incomings exceed his outgoings.'

When, in a large establishment, a housekeeper is kept, it will be advisable for the mistress to examine her accounts regularly. Then any increase of expenditure which may be apparent, can easily be explained, and the housekeeper will have the satisfaction of knowing whether her efforts to manage her department well and economically, have been successful.

Engaging domestics is one of those duties in which the judgment of the mistress must be keenly exercised. There are some respectable registry-offices, where good servants may sometimes be hired; but the plan rather to be recommended is, for the mistress to make inquiry amongst her circle of friends and acquaintances, and her tradespeople. The latter generally know those in their neighbourhood, who are wanting situations, and will communicate with them, when a personal interview with some of them will enable the mistress to form some idea of the characters of the applicants, and to suit herself accordingly.

We would here point out an error – and a grave one it is – into which some mistresses fall. They do not, when engaging a servant, expressly tell her all the duties which she will be expected to perform. This is an act of omission severely to be reprehended. Every portion of work which the maid will have to do, should be plainly stated by the mistress, and understood by the servant. If this plan is not carefully adhered to, domestic contention is almost certain to ensue, and this may not be easily settled; so that a change of servants, which is so much to be deprecated, is continually occurring.

In obtaining a servant's character, it is not well to be guided by a written one from some unknown quarter; but it is better to have an interview, if at all possible, with the former mistress. By this means you will be assisted in your decision of the suitableness of the servant for your place, from the appearance of the lady and the state of her house. Negligence and want of cleanliness in her and her household generally, will naturally lead you to the conclusion, that her servant has suffered from the influence of the bad example.

The proper course to pursue in order to obtain a personal interview with the lady is this: the servant in search of the situation must be desired to see her former mistress, and ask her to be kind enough to appoint a time, convenient to herself, when you may call on her; this proper observance of courtesy being necessary to prevent any unseasonable intrusion on the part of a stranger. Your first questions should be relative to the honesty and general morality of her former servant; and if no objection is stated in that respect, her other qualifications are then to be ascertained. Inquiries should be very minute, so that you may avoid disappointment and trouble, by knowing the weak points of your domestic.

The treatment of servants is of the highest possible moment, as well to the mistress as to the domestics themselves. On the head of the house the latter will naturally fix their attention; and if they perceive that the mistress's conduct is regulated by high and correct principles, they will not fail to respect her. If, also, a benevolent desire is shown to promote their comfort, at the same time that a steady performance of their duty is exacted, then their respect will not be unmingled with affection, and they will be still more solicitous to continue to deserve her favour.

[. . .]

The following table of the average yearly wages paid to domestics, with the various members of the household placed in the order in which they are usually ranked, will serve as a guide to regulate the expenditure of an establishment:

	When not found in Livery	*When found in Livery*
The House Steward	from £10–£80	—
The Valet	from £25–£50	from £20–£30
The Butler	from £25–£50	—
The Cook	from £20–£40	—
The Gardener	from £20–£40	—
The Footman	from £20–£40	from £15–£25
The Under Butler	from £15–£30	from £15–£25
The Coachman	—	from £20–£35
The Groom	from £15–£30	from £12–£20
The Under Footman	—	from £2–£20
The Page or Footboy	from £8–£18	from £6–£14
The Stableboy	from £6–£12	—

	When no extra allowance is made for tea, sugar and beer	*When an extra allowance is made for tea, sugar and beer*
The Housekeeper	from £20–£45	from £18–£40
The Lady's-maid	from £12–£25	from £10–£20
The Head Nurse	from £15–£30	from £13–£26
The Cook	from £11–£30	from £12–£26
The Upper Housemaid	from £12–£20	from £10–£17
The Upper Laundry-maid	from £12–£18	from £10–£15
The Maid-of-all-work	from £9–£14	from £7 10s.–£11
The Under Housemaid	from £8–£12	from £6 10s.–£10
The Still-room Maid	from £9–£14	from £8–£13
The Nursemaid	from £8–£12	from £5–£10
The Under Laundry-maid	from £9–£11	from £8–£12
The Kitchen-maid	from £9–£14	from £8–£12
The Scullery-maid	from £5–£9	from £4–£8

These quotations of wages are those usually given in or near the metropolis; but, of course, there are many circumstances connected with locality, and also having reference to the long service on the one hand, or the inexperience on the other, of domestics, which may render the wages still higher or lower than those named above. All the domestics mentioned in the above table would enter into the establishment of a wealthy nobleman. The number of servants, of course, would become smaller in proportion to the lesser size of the establishment; and we may here enumerate a scale of servants suited to various incomes, commencing with:

About £1,000 a year – A cook, upper housemaid, nursemaid, under housemaid, and a man servant
About £750 a year – A cook, housemaid, nursemaid, and footboy
About £500 a year – A cook, housemaid, and nursemaid
About £300 a year – A maid-of-all-work and nursemaid
About £200 or £150 a year – A maid-of-all-work (and girl occasionally)

Having thus indicated some of the more general duties of the mistress, relative to the moral government of her household, we will now give a few specific instructions on matters having a more practical relation to the position which she is supposed to occupy in the eye of the world. To do this the more clearly, we will begin with her earliest duties, and take her completely through the occupations of a day.

Having risen early, as we have already advised, and having given due attention to the bath, and made a careful toilet, it will be well at once to see that the children have received their proper ablutions, and are in every way clean and comfortable. The first meal of the day, breakfast, will then be served, at which all the family should be punctually present, unless illness, or other circumstances, prevent.

After breakfast is over, it will be well for the mistress to make a round of the kitchen and other offices, to see that all are in order, and that the morning's work has been properly performed by the various domestics. The orders for the day should then be given, and any questions which the domestics desire to ask, respecting their several departments, should be answered, and any special articles they may require, handed to them from the store-closet.

In those establishments where there is a housekeeper, it will not be so necessary for the mistress, personally, to perform the above-named duties.

After this general superintendence of her servants, the mistress, if a mother of a young family, may devote herself to the instruction of some of its younger members, or to the examination of the state of their wardrobe, leaving the later portion of the morning for reading, or for some amusing recreation. 'Recreation,' says Bishop Hall, 'is intended to the mind as whetting is to the scythe, to sharpen the edge of it, which would otherwise grow dull and blunt. He, therefore, that spends his whole time in recreation is ever whetting, never mowing; his grass may grow and his steed starve; as, contrarily, he that always toils and never recreates, is ever mowing, never whetting, labouring much to little purpose. As good no scythe as no edge. Then only doth the work go forward, when the scythe is so seasonably and moderately whetted that it may cut, and so cut, that it may have the help of sharpening.'

Unless the means of the mistress be very circumscribed, and she be obliged to devote a great deal of her time to the making of her children's clothes, and other economical pursuits, it is right that she should give some time to the pleasures of literature, the innocent delights of the garden, and to the improvement of any special abilities for music, painting, and other elegant arts, which she may, happily, possess.

These duties and pleasures being performed and enjoyed, the hour of luncheon will have arrived. This is a very necessary meal between an early breakfast and a late dinner, as a healthy person, with good exercise, should have a fresh supply of food once in four hours. It should be a light meal; but its solidity must, of course, be, in some degree, proportionate to the time it is intended to enable you to wait for your dinner, and the amount of exercise you take in the mean time. At this time, also, the servants' dinner will be served.

In those establishments where an early dinner is served, that will, of course, take the place of the luncheon. In many houses, where a nursery dinner is provided for the children and about one o'clock, the mistress and the elder portion of the family make their luncheon at the same time from the same joint, or whatever may be provided. A mistress will arrange, according to circumstances, the serving of the meal; but the more usual plan is for the lady of the house to have the joint brought to her table, and afterwards carried to the nursery.

After luncheon, morning calls and visits may be made and received. These may be divided under three heads: those of ceremony, friendship, and congratulation or condolence. Visits of ceremony, or courtesy, which occasionally merge into those of friendship, are to be paid under various circumstances. Thus, they are uniformly required after dining at a friend's house, or after a ball, picnic, or any other party. These visits should be short, a stay of from fifteen to twenty minutes being quite sufficient. A lady paying a visit may remove her boa or neckerchief; but neither her shawl nor bonnet.

When other visitors are announced, it is well to retire

as soon as possible, taking care to let it appear that their arrival is not the cause. When they are quietly seated, and the bustle of their entrance is over, rise from your chair, taking a kind leave of the hostess, and bowing politely to the guests. Should you call at an inconvenient time, not having ascertained the luncheon hour, or from any other inadvertence, retire as soon as possible, without, however, showing that you feel yourself an intruder. It is not difficult for any well-bred or even good-tempered person, to know what to say on such an occasion, and, on politely withdrawing, a promise can be made to call again; if the lady you have called on, appear really disappointed.

In paying visits of friendship, it will not be so necessary to be guided by etiquette as in paying visits of ceremony; and if a lady be pressed by her friend to remove her shawl and bonnet, it can be done if it will not interfere with her subsequent arrangements. It is, however, requisite to call at suitable times, and to avoid staying too long, if your friend is engaged. The courtesies of society should ever be maintained, even in the domestic circle, and amongst the nearest friends. During these visits, the manners should be easy and cheerful, and the subjects of conversation such as may be readily terminated. Serious discussions or arguments are to be altogether avoided, and there is much danger and impropriety in expressing opinions of those persons and characters with whom, perhaps, there is but a slight acquaintance.

It is not advisable, at any time, to take favourite dogs into another lady's drawing-room, for many persons have an absolute dislike to such animals; and besides this, there is always a chance of a breakage of some article occurring, through their leaping and bounding here and there, sometimes very much to the fear and annoyance of the hostess. Her children, also, unless they are particularly well-trained and orderly, and she is on exceedingly friendly terms with the hostess, should not accompany a lady in making morning calls. Where a lady, however, pays her visits in a carriage, the children can be taken in the vehicle, and remain in it until the visit is over.

For morning calls, it is well to be neatly attired; for a costume very different to that you generally wear, or anything approaching an evening dress, will be very much out of place. As a general rule, it may be said, both in reference to this and all other occasions, it is better to be under-dressed than over-dressed.

A strict account should be kept of ceremonial visits, and notice how soon your visits have been returned. An opinion may thus be formed as to whether your frequent visits are, or are not, desirable. There are, naturally, instances when the circumstances of old age or ill health will preclude any return of a call; but when this is the case, it must not interrupt the discharge of the duty.

In paying visits of condolence, it is to be remembered that they should be paid within a week after the event which occasions them. If the acquaintance, however, is but slight, then immediately after the family has appeared at public worship. A lady should send in her card, and if her friends be able to receive her, the visitor's manner and conversation should be subdued and in harmony with the character of her visit. Courtesy would dictate that a mourning card should be used, and that visitors, in paying condoling visits, should be dressed in black, either silk or plain-coloured apparel. Sympathy with the affliction of the family, is thus expressed, and these attentions are, in such cases, pleasing and soothing.

In all these visits, if your acquaintance or friend be not at home, a card should be left. If in a carriage, the servant will answer your inquiry and receive your card; if paying your visits on foot, give your card to the servant in the hall, but leave to go in and rest should on no account be asked. The form of words, 'Not at home', may be understood in different senses; but the only courteous way is to receive them as being perfectly true. You may imagine that the lady of the house is really at home, and that she would make an exception in your favour, or you may think that your acquaintance is not desired; but, in either case, not the slightest word is to escape you, which would suggest, on your part, such an impression.

In receiving morning calls, the foregoing description of the etiquette to be observed in paying them, will be of considerable service. It is to be added, however, that the occupations of drawing, music, or reading should be suspended on the entrance of morning visitors. If a lady, however, be engaged with light needlework, and none other is appropriate in the drawing-room, it may not be, under some circumstances, inconsistent with good breeding to quietly continue it during conversation, particularly if the visit be protracted, or the visitors be gentlemen.

Formerly the custom was to accompany all visitors

quitting the house to the door, and there take leave of them; but modern society, which has thrown off a great deal of this kind of ceremony, now merely requires that the lady of the house should rise from her seat, shake hands, or courtesy, in accordance with the intimacy she has with her guests, and ring the bell to summon the servant to attend them and open the door. In making a first call, either upon a newly-married couple, or persons newly arrived in the neighbourhood, a lady should leave her husband's card together with her own, at the same time, stating that the profession or business in which he is engaged has prevented him from having the pleasure of paying the visit, with her. It is a custom with many ladies, when on the eve of an absence from their neighbourhood, to leave on send their own and husband's cards, with the letters P. P. C. in the right-hand corner. These letters are the initials of the French words, 'Pour prendre congé,' meaning, 'To take leave'.

The morning calls being paid or received, and their etiquette properly attended to, the next great event of the day in most establishments is 'The Dinner' [. . .]

In giving or accepting an invitation for dinner, the following is the form of words generally made use of. They, however, can be varied in proportion to the intimacy or position of the hosts and guests:

> Mr and Mrs A— present their compliments to Mr and Mrs B—, and request the honour, [or hope to have the pleasure] of their company to dinner on Wednesday, the 6th of December next.
>
> A— Street, November 13th, 1859. R.S.V.P.

The letters in the corner imply 'Répondez, s'il vous plaît'; meaning, 'an answer will oblige'. The reply, accepting the invitation, is couched in the following terms:

> Mr and Mrs B— present their compliments to Mr and Mrs A—, and will do themselves the honour of, [or will have much pleasure in] accepting their kind invitation to dinner on the 6th of December next.
>
> B— Square, November 18th, 1859.

Cards, or invitations for a dinner-party, should be issued a fortnight or three weeks (sometimes even a month) beforehand, and care should be taken by the hostess, in the selection of the invited guests, that they should be suited to each other. Much also of the pleasure of a dinner-party will depend on the arrangement of the guests at table, so as to form a due admixture of talkers and listeners, the grave and the gay. If an invitation to dinner is accepted, the guests should be punctual, and the mistress ready in her drawing-room to receive them. At some periods it has been considered fashionable to come late to dinner, but lately nous avons changé tout cela.

The half-hour before dinner has always been considered as the great ordeal through which the mistress, in giving a dinner-party, will either pass with flying colours, or, lose many of her laurels. The anxiety to receive her guests – her hope that all will be present in due time – her trust in the skill of her cook, and the attention of the other domestics, all tend to make these few minutes a trying time. The mistress, however, must display no kind of agitation, but show her tact in suggesting light and cheerful subjects of conversation, which will be much aided by the introduction of any particular new book, curiosity of art, or article of vertu, which may pleasantly engage the attention of the company. 'Waiting for Dinner', however, is a trying time, and there are few who have not felt:

> How sad it is to sit and pine,
> The long half-hour before we dine!
> Upon our watches oft to look,
> Then wonder at the clock and cook . . .
> And strive to laugh in spite of Fate!
> But laughter forced soon quits the room,
> And leaves it in its former gloom.
> But lo! the dinner now appears,
> The object of our hopes and fears,
> The end of all our pain!

In giving an entertainment of this kind, the mistress should remember that it is her duty to make her guests feel happy, comfortable, and quite at their ease; and the guests should also consider that they have come to the house of their hostess to be happy. Thus an opportunity is given to all for innocent enjoyment and intellectual improvement, when also acquaintances may be formed that may prove invaluable through life, and information gained that will enlarge the mind. Many celebrated men and women have been great talkers; and, amongst others, the genial Sir Walter Scott, who spoke freely to every one, and a favourite remark of whom it was, that he never did so without learning something he didn't know before.

Dinner being announced, the host offers his arm to, and places on his right hand at the dinner-table, the lady to whom he desires to pay most respect, either on account of her age, position, or from her being the greatest stranger in the party. If this lady be married and her husband present, the latter takes the hostess to her place at table, and seats himself at her right hand. The rest of the company follow in couples, as specified by the master and mistress of the house, arranging the party according to their rank and other circumstances which may be known to the host and hostess.

It will be found of great assistance to the placing of a party at the dinner-table, to have the names of the guests neatly (and correctly) written on small cards, and placed at that part of the table where it is desired they should sit. With respect to the number of guests, it has often been said, that a private dinner-party should consist of not less than the number of the Graces, or more than that of the Muses. A party of ten or twelve is, perhaps, in a general way, sufficient to enjoy themselves and be enjoyed. White kid gloves are worn by ladies at dinner-parties, but should be taken off before the business of dining commences.

The guests being seated at the dinner-table, the lady begins to help the soup, which is handed round, commencing with the gentleman on her right and on her left, and continuing in the same order till all are served. It is generally established as a rule, not to ask for soup or fish twice, as, in so doing, part of the company may be kept waiting too long for the second course, when, perhaps, a little revenge is taken by looking at the awkward consumer of a second portion. This rule, however, may, under various circumstances, not be considered as binding.

It is not usual, where taking wine is *en règle*, for a gentleman to ask a lady to take wine until the fish or soup is finished, and then the gentleman honoured by sitting on the right of the hostess, may politely inquire if she will do him the honour of taking wine with him. This will act as a signal to the rest of the company, the gentleman of the house most probably requesting the same pleasure of the ladies at his right and left. At many tables, however, the custom or fashion of drinking wine in this manner, is abolished, and the servant fills the glasses of the guests with the various wines suited to the course which is in progress.

When dinner is finished, the dessert is placed on the table, accompanied with finger-glasses. It is the custom of some gentlemen to wet a corner of the napkin; but the hostess, whose behaviour will set the tone to all the ladies present, will merely wet the tips of her fingers, which will serve all the purposes required. The French and other continentals have a habit of gargling the mouth; but it is a custom which no English gentlewoman should, in the slightest degree, imitate.

When fruit has been taken, and a glass or two of wine passed round, the time will have arrived when the hostess will rise, and thus give the signal for the ladies to leave the gentlemen, and retire to the drawing-room. The gentlemen of the party will rise at the same time, and he who is nearest the door, will open it for the ladies, all remaining courteously standing until the last lady has withdrawn. Dr Johnson has a curious paragraph on the effects of a dinner on men. 'Before dinner,' he says, 'men meet with great inequality of understanding; and those who are conscious of their inferiority have the modesty not to talk. When they have drunk wine, every man feels himself happy, and loses that modesty, and grows impudent and vociferous; but he is not improved, he is only not sensible of his defects.' This is rather severe, but there may be truth in it.

In former times, when the bottle circulated freely amongst the guests, it was necessary for the ladies to retire earlier than they do at present, for the gentlemen of the company soon became unfit to conduct themselves with that decorum which is essential in the presence of ladies. Thanks, however, to the improvements in modern society, and the high example shown to the nation by its most illustrious personages, temperance is, in these happy days, a striking feature in the character of a gentleman. Delicacy of conduct towards the female sex has increased with the esteem in which they are now universally held, and thus, the very early withdrawing of the ladies from the dining-room is to be deprecated. A lull in the conversation will seasonably indicate the moment for the ladies' departure.

After-dinner invitations may be given; by which we wish to be understood, invitations for the evening. The time of the arrival of these visitors will vary according to their engagements, or sometimes will be varied in obedience to the caprices of fashion. Guests invited for the evening are, however, generally considered at liberty to arrive whenever it will best suit themselves – usually between nine and twelve, unless earlier hours are specifically named. By this arrangement, many fashionable people and others, who have numerous engagements to fulfil, often contrive to make their appearance at two or three parties in the course of one evening.

The etiquette of the dinner-party table being disposed of, let us now enter slightly into that of an evening party or ball. The invitations issued and accepted for either of these, will be written in the same style as those already described for a dinner-party. They should be sent out at least three weeks before the day fixed for the event, and should be replied to within a week of their receipt [. . .]

As the ladies and gentlemen arrive, each should be shown to a room exclusively provided for their reception; and in that set apart for the ladies, attendants should be in waiting to assist in uncloaking, and helping to arrange the hair and toilet of those who require it. It will be found convenient, in those cases where the number of guests is large, to provide numbered tickets, so that they can be attached to the cloaks and shawls of each lady, a duplicate of which should be handed to the guest. Coffee is sometimes provided in this, or an anteroom, for those who would like to partake of it.

As the visitors are announced by the servant, it is not necessary for the lady of the house to advance each time towards the door, but merely to rise from her seat to receive their courtesies and congratulations. If, indeed, the hostess wishes to show particular favour to some peculiarly honoured guests, she may introduce them to others, whose acquaintance she may imagine will be especially suitable and agreeable. It is very often the practice of the master of the house to introduce one gentleman to another, but occasionally the lady performs this office; when it will, of course, be polite for the persons thus introduced to take their seats together for the time being.

The custom of non-introduction is very much in vogue in many houses, and guests are thus left to discover for themselves the position and qualities of the people around them. The servant, indeed, calls out the names of all the visitors as they arrive, but, in many instances, mispronounces them; so that it will not be well to follow this information, as if it were an unerring guide. In our opinion, it is a cheerless and depressing custom, although, in thus speaking, we do not allude to the large assemblies of the aristocracy, but to the smaller parties of the middle classes.

A separate room or convenient buffet should be appropriated for refreshments, and to which the dancers may retire; and cakes and biscuits, with wine negus, lemonade, and ices, handed round. A supper is also mostly provided at the private parties of the middle classes; and this requires, on the part of the hostess, a great deal of attention and supervision. It usually takes place between the first and second parts of the programme of the dances, of which there should be several prettily written or printed copies distributed about the ball-room.

In private parties, a lady is not to refuse the invitation of a gentleman to dance, unless she be previously engaged.

The hostess must be supposed to have asked to her house only those persons whom she knows to be perfectly respectable and of unblemished character, as well as pretty equal in position; and thus, to decline the offer of any gentleman present, would be a tacit reflection on the master and mistress of the house. It may be mentioned here, more especially for the young who will read this book, that introductions at balls or evening parties, cease with the occasion that calls them forth, no introduction, at these times, giving a gentleman a right to address, afterwards, a lady. She is, consequently, free, next morning, to pass her partner at a ball of the previous evening without the slightest recognition.

The ball is generally opened, that is, the first place in the first quadrille is occupied, by the lady of the house. When anything prevents this, the host will usually lead off the dance with the lady who is either the highest in rank, or the greatest stranger. It will be well for the hostess, even if she be very partial to the amusement, and a graceful dancer, not to participate in it to any great extent, lest her lady guests should have occasion to complain of her monopoly of the gentlemen, and other causes of neglect. A few dances will suffice to show her interest in the entertainment, without unduly trenching on the attention due to her guests. In all its parts a ball should be perfect:

> The music, and the banquet, and the wine;
> The garlands, the rose-odours, and the flowers.

The hostess or host, during the progress of a ball, will courteously accost and chat with their friends, and take care that the ladies are furnished with seats, and that those who wish to dance are provided with partners. A gentle hint from the hostess, conveyed in a quiet lady-like manner, that certain ladies have remained unengaged during several dances, is sure not to be neglected by any gentleman. Thus will be studied the comfort and enjoyment of the guests, and no lady, in leaving the house, will be able to feel the chagrin and disappointment of not having been invited to 'stand up' in a dance during the whole of the evening.

When any of the carriages of the guests are announced, or the time for their departure arrived, they should make a slight intimation to the hostess, without, however, exciting any observation, that they are about to depart. If this cannot be done, however, without creating too much bustle, it will be better for the visitors to retire quietly without taking their leave. During the course of the week, the hostess will expect to receive from every guest a call, where it is possible, or cards expressing the gratification experienced from her entertainment. This attention is due to every lady for the pains and trouble she has been at, and tends to promote social, kindly feelings.

Having thus discoursed of parties of pleasure, it will be an interesting change to return to the more domestic business of the house, although all the details we have been giving of dinner-parties, balls, and the like, appertain to the department of the mistress. Without a knowledge of the etiquette to be observed on these occasions, a mistress would be unable to enjoy and appreciate those friendly pleasant meetings which give, as it were, a fillip to life, and make the quiet happy home of an English gentlewoman appear the more delightful and enjoyable. [. . .]

Of the manner of passing evenings at home, there is none pleasanter than in such recreative enjoyments as those which relax the mind from its severer duties, whilst they stimulate it with a gentle delight. Where there are young people forming a part of the evening circle, interesting and agreeable pastime should especially be promoted. It is of incalculable benefit to them that their homes should possess all the attractions of healthful amusement, comfort, and happiness; for if they do not find pleasure there, they will seek it elsewhere. It ought, therefore, to enter into the domestic policy of every parent, to make her children feel that home is the happiest place in the world; that to imbue them with this delicious home-feeling is one of the choicest gifts a parent can bestow.

Light or fancy needlework often forms a portion of the evening's recreation for the ladies of the household, and this may be varied by an occasional game at chess or backgammon. It has often been remarked, too, that nothing is more delightful to the feminine members of a family, than the reading aloud of some good standard work or amusing publication. A knowledge of polite literature may be thus obtained by the whole family, especially if the reader is able and willing to explain the more difficult passages of the book, and expatiate on the wisdom and beauties it may contain. This plan, in a great measure, realizes the advice of Lord Bacon, who says, 'Read not to contradict and refute, nor to believe and take for granted, nor to find talk and discourse, but to weigh and consider.'

In retiring for the night, it is well to remember that early rising is almost impossible, if late going to bed be the order, or rather disorder, of the house. The younger members of a family should go early and at regular hours to their beds, and the domestics as soon as possible after a reasonably appointed hour. Either the master or the mistress of a house should, after all have gone to their separate rooms, see that all is right with respect to the lights and fires below; and no servants should, on any account, be allowed to remain up after the heads of the house have retired.

[. . .]

Such are the onerous duties which enter into the position of the mistress of a house, and such are, happily, with a slight but continued attention, of by no means difficult performance. She ought always to remember that she is the first and the last, the Alpha and the Omega in the government of her establishment; and that it is by her conduct that its whole internal policy is regulated. She is, therefore, a person of far more importance in a community than she usually thinks she is. On her pattern her daughters model themselves; by her counsels they are directed; through her virtues all are honoured; – 'her children rise up and call her blessed; her husband, also, and he praiseth her.' Therefore, let each mistress always remember her responsible position, never approving a mean action, nor speaking an unrefined word. Let her conduct be such that her inferiors may respect her, and such as an honourable and right-minded man may look for in his wife and the mother of his children. Let her think of the many compliments and the sincere homage that have been paid to her sex by the greatest philosophers and writers, both in ancient and modern times. Let her not forget that she has to show herself worthy of Campbell's compliment when he said:

> The world was sad! the garden was a wild!
> And man the hermit sigh'd, till woman smiled.

Let her prove herself, then, the happy companion of man, and able to take unto herself the praises of the pious prelate, Jeremy Taylor, who says: 'A good wife is Heaven's last best gift to man – his angel and minister of graces innumerable – his gem of many virtues – his casket of jewels – her voice is sweet music – her smiles his brightest day; her kiss, the guardian of his innocence; her arms, the pale of his safety, the balm of his health, the balsam of his life; her industry, his surest wealth; her economy, his safest steward; her lips, his faithful counsellors; her bosom, the softest pillow of his cares; and her prayers, the ablest advocates of Heaven's blessings on his head.'

Cherishing, then, in her breast the respected utterances of the good and the great, let the mistress of every house rise to the responsibility of its management; so that, in doing her duty to all around her, she may receive the genuine reward of respect, love, and affection!

Recipes for Soup

APPLE SOUP

Ingredients – 2 lb. of good boiling apples, ¾ teaspoonful of white pepper, 6 cloves, cayenne or ginger to taste, 3 quarts of medium stock.
Mode – Peel and quarter the apples, taking out their cores; put them into the stock, stew them gently till tender. Rub the whole through a strainer, add the seasoning, give it one boil up, and serve.
Time – 1 hour. *Average cost* – per quart, 1*s*.
Seasonable – from September to December.
Sufficient for 10 persons.

CARROT SOUP

Ingredients – 2 lb. of carrots, 3 oz. of butter, seasoning to taste of salt and cayenne, 2 quarts of stock or gravy soup.
Mode – Scrape and cut out all specks from the carrots, wash, and wipe them dry, and then reduce them into quarter-inch slices. Put the butter into a large stewpan, and when it is melted, add 2 lb. of the sliced carrots, and let them stew gently for an hour without browning. Add to them the soup, and allow them to simmer till tender – say for nearly an hour. Press them through a strainer with the soup, and add salt and cayenne if required. Boil

the whole gently for 5 minutes, skim well, and serve as hot as possible.

Time – 1¼ hour. *Average cost* – per quart, 1*s*. 1*d*.

The Carrot

There is a wild carrot which grows in England; but it is white and small, and not much esteemed. The garden carrot in general use, was introduced in the reign of Queen Elizabeth, and was, at first, so highly esteemed, that the ladies wore leaves of it in their head-dresses. It is of great value in the culinary art, especially for soups and stews. It can be used also for beer instead of malt, and, in distillation, it yields a large quantity of spirit. The carrot is proportionably valuable as it has more of the red than the yellow part. There is a large red variety much used by the farmers for colouring butter. As a garden vegetable, it is what is called the orange-carrot that is usually cultivated. As a fattening food for cattle, it is excellent; but for man it is indigestible, on account of its fibrous matter. Of 1,000 parts, 95 consist of sugar, and 3 of starch.

USEFUL SOUP FOR BENEVOLENT PURPOSES

Ingredients – An ox-cheek, any pieces of trimmings of beef, which may be bought very cheaply (say 4 lb.), a few bones, any pot-liquor the larder may furnish, ¼ peck of onions, 6 leeks, a large bunch of herbs, ½ lb. of celery (the outside pieces, or green tops, do very well); ½ lb. of carrots, ½ lb. of turnips, ½ lb. of coarse brown sugar, ½ a pint of beer, 4 lb. of common rice, or pearl barley; ½ lb. of salt,

1 oz. of black pepper, a few raspings, 10 gallons of water.
Mode – Cut up the meat in small pieces, break the bones, put them in a copper, with the 10 gallons of water, and stew for ½ an hour. Cut up the vegetables, put them in with the sugar and beer, and boil for 4 hours. Two hours before the soup is wanted, add the rice and raspings, and keep stirring till it is well mixed in the soup, which simmer gently. If the liquor reduces too much, fill up with water.
Time – 6½ hours.
Average cost – 1½ *d.* per quart.
Note – The above recipe was used in the winter of 1858 by the Editress, who made, each week, in her copper, 8 or 9 gallons of this soup, for distribution amongst about a dozen families of the village near which she lives. The cost, as will be seen, was not great; but she has reason to believe that the soup was very much liked, and gave to the members of those families, a dish of warm, comforting food, in place of the cold meat and piece of bread which form, with too many cottagers, their usual meal, when, with a little more knowledge of the 'cooking' art, they might have, for less expense, a warm dish, every day.

HARE SOUP

Ingredients – A hare fresh-killed, 1 lb. of lean gravy-beef, a slice of ham, 1 carrot, 2 onions, a faggot of savoury herbs, ¼ oz. of whole black pepper, a little browned flour, ¼ pint of port wine, the crumb of two French rolls, salt and cayenne to taste, 3 quarts of water.
Mode – Skin and paunch the hare, saving the liver and as

much blood as possible. Cut it in pieces, and put it in a stewpan with all the ingredients, and simmer gently for 8 hours. This soup should be made the day before it is wanted. Strain through a sieve, put the best parts of the hare in the soup, and serve.

[. . .]

Time – 8 hours. *Average cost* – 1*s*. 9*d*. per quart.
Seasonable – from September to February.
Sufficient for 10 persons.

Recipes for Fish

STEWED EELS

Ingredients – 2 lb. of eels, 1 pint of rich strong stock, 1 onion, 3 cloves, a piece of lemon-peel, 1 glass of port or Madeira, 3 tablespoonfuls of cream; thickening of flour; cayenne and lemon-juice to taste.
Mode – Wash and skin the eels, and cut them into pieces about 3 inches long; pepper and salt them, and lay them in a stewpan; pour over the stock, add the onion stuck with cloves, the lemon-peel, and the wine. Stew gently for ½ hour, or rather more, and lift them carefully on a dish, which keep hot. Strain the gravy, stir to the cream sufficient flour to thicken; mix altogether, boil for 2 minutes, and add the cayenne and lemon-juice; pour over the eels and serve.
Time – ¾ hour. *Average cost* for this quantity, 2*s.* 3*d.* *Seasonable* – from June to March. Sufficient for 5 or 6 persons.

The Common Eel

This fish is known frequently to quit its native element, and to set off on a wandering expedition in the night, or just about the close of day, over the meadows, in search of snails and other prey. It also, sometimes, betakes itself to isolated ponds, apparently for no other pleasure than that which may be supposed to be found in a change of habitation. This, of course, accounts for eels being found in waters which were never suspected to contain them. This rambling disposition in the eel has been long known to naturalists, and, from the following lines, it seems to have been known to the ancients:

> Thus the mail'd tortoise, and the wand'ring eel,
> Oft to the neighbouring beach will silent steal.

The Lamprey

With the Romans, this fish occupied a respectable rank among the piscine tribes, and in Britain it has at various periods stood high in public favour. It was the cause of the death of Henry I of England, who ate so much of them, that it brought on an attack of indigestion, which carried him off. It is an inhabitant of the sea, ascending rivers, principally about the end of winter, and, after passing a few months in fresh water, returning again to its oceanic residence. It is most in season in March, April, and May, but is, by some, regarded as an unwholesome food, although looked on by others as a great delicacy. They are dressed as eels.

FISH AND OYSTER PIE

Ingredients – Any remains of cold fish, such as cod or haddock; 2 dozen oysters, pepper and salt to taste, bread crumbs sufficient for the quantity of fish; ½ teaspoonful of grated nutmeg, 1 teaspoonful of finely-chopped parsley.
Mode – Clear the fish from the bones, and put a layer of it in a pie-dish, which sprinkle with pepper and salt;

then a layer of bread crumbs, oysters, nutmeg, and chopped parsley. Repeat this till the dish is quite full. You may form a covering either of bread crumbs, which should be browned, or puff-paste, which should be cut into long strips, and laid in cross-bars over the fish, with a line of the paste first laid round the edge. Before putting on the top, pour in some made melted butter, or a little thin white sauce, and the oyster-liquor, and bake.
Time – If made of cooked fish, ¼ hour; if made of fresh fish and puff-paste, ¾ hour.
Average cost – 1*s*. 6*d*.
Seasonable – from September to April.
Note – A nice little dish may be made by flaking any cold fish, adding a few oysters, seasoning with pepper and salt, and covering with mashed potatoes; ¼ hour will bake it.

LOBSTER
À la mode Française

Ingredients – 1 lobster, 4 tablespoonfuls of white stock, 2 tablespoonfuls of cream, pounded mace, and cayenne to taste; bread crumbs.
Mode – Pick the meat from the shell, and cut it up into small square pieces; put the stock, cream, and seasoning into a stewpan, add the lobster, and let it simmer gently for 6 minutes. Serve it in the shell, which must be nicely cleaned, and have a border of puff-paste; cover it with bread crumbs, place small pieces of butter over, and brown before the fire, or with a salamander.
Time – ¼ hour. *Average cost* – 2*s*. 6*d*. *Seasonable* – at any time.

Celerity of the Lobster

In its element, the lobster is able to run with great speed upon its legs, or small claws, and, if alarmed, to spring, tail foremost, to a considerable distance, 'even', it is said, 'with the swiftness of a bird flying'. Fishermen have seen some of them pass about thirty feet with a wonderful degree of swiftness. When frightened, they will take their spring, and, like a chamois of the Alps, plant themselves upon the very spot upon which they designed to hold themselves.

FRIED OYSTERS

Ingredients – 3 dozen oysters, 2 oz. butter, 1 tablespoonful of ketchup, a little chopped lemon-peel, ½ teaspoonful of chopped parsley.
Mode – Boil the oysters for 1 minute in their own liquor, and drain them; fry them with the butter, ketchup, lemon-peel, and parsley; lay them on a dish, and garnish with fried potatoes, toasted sippets, and parsley. This is a delicious delicacy, and is a favourite Italian dish.
Time – 5 minutes. *Average cost* for this quantity, 1*s*. 9*d*.
Seasonable – from September to April.
Sufficient for 4 persons.

ADDENDUM AND ANECDOTE

[. . .] As to which is the best fish, there has been much discussion. The old Latin proverb, however, de gustibus non disputandum, and the more modern Spanish one, sobre los gustos no hai disputa, declare, with equal force, that where taste is concerned, no decision can be arrived at. Each person's palate may be differently affected – pleased or displeased; and there is no standard by which to judge why a red mullet, a sole, or a turbot, should be better or worse than a salmon, trout, pike, or a tiny tench [. . .]

In Brillat-Savarin's clever and amusing volume *The Physiology of Taste*, he says, that towards the end of the eighteenth century it was a most common thing for a well-arranged entertainment in Paris to commence with oysters, and that many guests were not contented without swallowing twelve dozen. Being anxious to know the weight of this advanced-guard, he ascertained that a dozen oysters, fluid included, weighed 4 ounces – thus, the twelve dozen would weigh about 3 lbs.; and there can be no doubt, that the same persons who made no worse a dinner on account of having partaken of the oysters, would have been completely satisfied if they had eaten the same weight of chicken or mutton. An anecdote, perfectly well authenticated, is narrated of a French gentleman (Monsieur Laperte), residing at Versailles, who was extravagantly fond of oysters, declaring he never had enough. Savarin resolved to procure him the satisfaction, and gave him an invitation to dinner, which was duly accepted. The guest arrived, and his host kept company with him in swallowing the delicious bivalves up to the tenth dozen, when, exhausted, he gave up, and let Monsieur Laperte go on alone. This gentleman managed to eat thirty-two dozen within an hour, and would doubtless have got through more, but the person who opened them is described as not being very skilful. In the interim Savarin was idle, and at length, tired with his painful state of inaction, he said to Laperte, whilst the latter was still in full career, 'Mon cher, you will not eat as many oysters today as you meant; let us dine.' They dined, and the insatiable oyster-eater acted at the repast as if he had fasted for a week.

Recipes for Sauces, Pickles and Gravies

An anecdote is told of the prince de Soubise, who, intending to give an entertainment, asked for the bill of fare. His chef came, presenting a list adorned with vignettes, and the first article of which, that met the prince's eye, was 'fifty hams'. 'Bertrand,' said the prince, 'I think you must be extravagant; Fifty hams! do you intend to feast my whole regiment?' 'No, Prince, there will be but one on the table, and the surplus I need for my Espagnole, blondes, garnitures, etc.' 'Bertrand, you are robbing me: this item will not do.' 'Monseigneur,' said the artiste, 'you do not appreciate me. Give me the order, and I will put those fifty hams in a crystal flask no longer than my thumb.' The prince smiled, and the hams were passed. This was all very well for the prince de Soubise; but as we do not write for princes and nobles alone, but that our British sisters may make the best dishes out of the least expensive ingredients, we will also pass the hams, and give a few general directions concerning Sauces, etc.

BENGAL RECIPE FOR MAKING MANGO CHETNEY

Ingredients – 1½ lb. of moist sugar, ¾ lb. of salt, ¼ lb. of garlic, ¼ lb. of onions, ¾ lb. of powdered ginger, ¼ lb. of dried chilies, ¾ lb. of mustard-seed, ¾ lb. of stoned raisins, 2 bottles of best vinegar, 30 large unripe sour apples. *Mode* – The sugar must be made into syrup; the garlic, onions, and ginger be finely pounded in a mortar; the mustard-seed be washed in cold vinegar, and dried in the sun; the apples be peeled, cored, and sliced, and boiled in a bottle and a half of the vinegar. When all this is done, and the apples are quite cold, put them into a large pan, and gradually mix the whole of the rest of the ingredients, including the remaining half-bottle of vinegar. It must be well stirred until the whole is thoroughly blended, and then put into bottles for use. Tie a piece of wet bladder over the mouths of the bottles, after they are well corked. This chetney is very superior to any which can be bought, and one trial will prove it to be delicious.

Note – This recipe was given by a native to an English lady, who had long been a resident in India, and who, since her return to her native country, has become quite celebrated amongst her friends for the excellence of this Eastern relish.

Garlic

The smell of this plant is generally considered offensive, and it is the most acrimonious in its taste of the whole of the alliaceous tribe. In 1548 it was introduced to England from the shores of the Mediterranean, where it is abundant, and in Sicily it grows naturally. It was in greater repute with our ancestors than it is with ourselves, although it is still used as a seasoning herb. On the continent, especially in Italy, it is much used, and the French consider it an essential in many made dishes.

GREEN SAUCE FOR GREEN GEESE OR DUCKLINGS

Ingredients – ¼ pint of sorrel-juice, 1 glass of sherry, ½ pint of green gooseberries, 1 teaspoonful of pounded sugar, 1 oz. of fresh butter.
Mode – Boil the gooseberries in water until they are quite tender; mash them and press them through a sieve; put the pulp into a saucepan with the above ingredients; simmer for 3 or 4 minutes, and serve very hot.
Time – 3 or 4 minutes.
Note – We have given this recipe as a sauce for green geese, thinking that some of our readers might sometimes require it; but, at the generality of fashionable tables, it is now seldom or never served.

Sauces and Gravies in the Middle Ages

Neither poultry, butcher's meat, nor roast game were eaten dry in the middle ages, any more than fried fish is now. Different sauces, each having its own peculiar flavour, were served with all these dishes, and even with the various parts of each animal. Strange and grotesque sauces, as, for example, 'eggs cooked on the spit,' 'butter fried and roasted,' were invented by the cooks of those days; but these preparations had hardly any other merit than that of being surprising and difficult to make.

A QUICKLY-MADE GRAVY

Ingredients – ½ lb. of shin of beef, ½ onion, ¼ carrot, 2 or 3 sprigs of parsley and savoury herbs, a piece of butter about the size of a walnut; cayenne and mace to taste, ¾ pint of water.

Mode – Cut up the meat into very small pieces, slice the onion and carrot, and put them into a small saucepan with the butter. Keep stirring over a sharp fire until they have taken a little colour, when add the water and the remaining ingredients. Simmer for ½ hour, skim well, strain, and flavour, when it will be ready for use.

Time – ½ hour. *Average cost* – for this quantity, 5*d*.

A Hundred Different Dishes

Modern housewives know pretty well how much care, and attention, and foresight are necessary in order to serve well a little dinner for six or eight persons – a dinner which will give credit to the ménage, and satisfaction and pleasure to the guests. A quickly-made gravy, under some circumstances that we have known occur, will be useful to many housekeepers when they have not much time for preparation. But, talking of speed, and time, and preparation, what a combination of all these must have been necessary for the feast at the wedding of Charles VI of France. On that occasion, as Froissart the chronicler tells us, the art of cooking, with its innumerable paraphernalia of sauces, with gravy, pepper, cinnamon, garlic, scallion, brains, gravy soups, milk potage, and ragoûts, had a signal triumph. The skilful chef-de-cuisine of the royal household covered the great marble table of the regal palace with no less than a hundred different dishes, prepared in a hundred different ways.

INDIAN MUSTARD

An excellent relish to bread and butter, or any cold meat

Ingredients – ¼ lb. of the best mustard, ¼ lb. of flour, ½ oz. of salt, 4 shalots, 4 tablespoonfuls of vinegar, 4 tablespoonfuls of ketchup, ¼ bottle of anchovy sauce.
Mode – Put the mustard, flour, and salt into a basin, and make them into a stiff paste with boiling water. Boil the shalots with the vinegar, ketchup, and anchovy sauce, for 10 minutes, and pour the whole, boiling, over the mixture in the basin; stir well, and reduce it to a proper thickness; put it into a bottle, with a bruised shalot at the bottom, and store away for use. This makes an excellent relish, and if properly prepared will keep for years.

Mustard

Before the year 1729, mustard was not known at English tables. About that time an old woman, of the name of Clements, residing in Durham, began to grind the seed in a mill, and to pass the flour through several processes necessary to free the seed from its husks. She kept her secret for many years to herself, during which she sold large quantities of mustard throughout the country, but especially in London. Here it was introduced to the royal table, when it received the approval of George I. From the circumstance of Mrs Clements being a resident at Durham, it obtained the name of Durham mustard. In the county of that name it is still principally cultivated, and the plant is remarkable for the rapidity of its growth. It is the best stimulant employed to impart strength to the digestive organs, and even in its previously coarsely-pounded state, had a high reputation with our ancestors.

OYSTER KETCHUP

Ingredients – Sufficient oysters to fill a pint measure, 1 pint of sherry, 3 oz. of salt, 1 drachm of cayenne, 2 drachms of pounded mace.
Mode – Procure the oysters very fresh, and open sufficient to fill a pint measure; save the liquor, and scald the oysters in it with the sherry; strain the oysters, and put them in a mortar with the salt, cayenne, and mace; pound the whole until reduced to a pulp, then add it to the liquor in which they were scalded; boil it again five minutes, and skim well; rub the whole through a sieve, and, when cold, bottle and cork closely. The corks should be sealed.
Seasonable – from September to April.
Note – Cider may be substituted for the sherry.

SALAD DRESSING
Excellent

Ingredients – 1 teaspoonful of mixed mustard, 1 teaspoonful of pounded sugar, 2 tablespoonfuls of salad oil, 4 tablespoonfuls of milk, 2 tablespoonfuls of vinegar, cayenne and salt to taste.
Mode – Put the mixed mustard into a salad-bowl with the sugar, and add the oil drop by drop, carefully stirring

and mixing all these ingredients well together. Proceed in this manner with the milk and vinegar, which must be added very gradually, or the sauce will curdle. Put in the seasoning, when the mixture will be ready for use. If this dressing is properly made, it will have a soft creamy appearance, and will be found very delicious with crab, or cold fried fish (the latter cut into dice), as well as with salads. In mixing salad dressings, the ingredients cannot be added too gradually, or stirred too much.
Average cost – for this quantity, 3*d*. Sufficient for a small salad.

This recipe can be confidently recommended by the editress, to whom it was given by an intimate friend noted for her salads.

Scarcity of Salads in England

Three centuries ago, very few vegetables were cultivated in England, and an author writing of the period of Henry VIII's reign, tells us that neither salad, nor carrots, nor cabbages, nor radishes, nor any other comestibles of a like nature, were grown in any part of the kingdom: they came from Holland and Flanders. We further learn, that Queen Catharine herself, with all her royalty, could not procure a salad of English growth for her dinner. The king was obliged to mend this sad state of affairs, and send to Holland for a gardener in order to cultivate those pot-herbs, in the growth of which England is now, perhaps, not behind any other country in Europe.

Recipes for Beef

BUBBLE-AND-SQUEAK

Cold meat cookery

Ingredients – A few thin slices of cold boiled beef, butter, cabbage, 1 sliced onion, pepper and salt to taste.
Mode – Fry the slices of beef gently in a little butter, taking care not to dry them up. Lay them on a flat dish, and cover with fried greens. The greens may be prepared from cabbage sprouts or green savoys. They should be boiled till tender, well drained, minced, and placed, till quite hot, in a frying-pan, with butter, a sliced onion, and seasoning of pepper and salt. When the onion is done, it is ready to serve.
Time – Altogether, ½ hour.
Average cost – exclusive of the cold beef, 3*d*.
Seasonable – at any time.

FRIED OX-FEET OR COW-HEEL

Ingredients – Ox-feet, the yolk of 1 egg, bread crumbs, parsley, salt and cayenne to taste, boiling butter.
Mode – Wash, scald, and thoroughly clean the feet, and cut them into pieces about 2 inches long; have ready some fine bread crumbs mixed with a little minced parsley, cayenne, and salt; dip the pieces of heel into the yolk

of egg, sprinkle them with the bread crumbs, and fry them until of a nice brown in boiling butter.
Time – 1 hour. *Average cost* – 6*d*. each.
Seasonable – at any time.
Note – Ox-feet may be dressed in various ways, stewed in gravy or plainly boiled and served with melted butter. When plainly boiled, the liquor will answer for making sweet or relishing jellies, and also to give richness to soups or gravies.

BRISKET OF BEEF, À LA FLAMANDE

Ingredients – About 6 or 8 lb. of the brisket of beef, 4 or 5 slices of bacon, 2 carrots, 1 onion, a bunch of savoury herbs, salt and pepper to taste, 4 cloves, 4 whole allspice, 2 blades of mace.
Mode – Choose that portion of the brisket which contains the gristle, trim it, and put it into a stewpan with the slices of bacon, which should be put under and over the meat. Add the vegetables, herbs, spices, and seasoning, and cover with a little weak stock or water; close the stewpan as hermetically as possible, and simmer very gently for 4 hours. Strain the liquor, reserve a portion of it for sauce, and the remainder boil quickly over a sharp fire until reduced to a glaze, with which glaze the meat. Garnish the dish with scooped carrots and turnips, and when liked, a little cabbage; all of which must be cooked separately. Thicken and flavour the liquor that was saved for sauce, pour it round the meat, and serve. The beef may also be garnished with glazed onions, artichoke-bottoms, etc.

Time – 4 hours. *Average cost* – 7*d*. per lb.
Sufficient for 6 or 8 persons.
Seasonable – at any time.

French Beef

It has been all but universally admitted, that the beef of France is greatly inferior in quality to that of England, owing to inferiority of pasturage. Monsieur Curmer, however, one of the latest writers on the culinary art, tells us that this is a vulgar error, and that French beef is far superior to that of England. This is mere vaunting on the part of our neighbours, who seem to want *la gloire* in everything; and we should not deign to notice it, if it had occurred in a work of small pretensions; but Monsieur Curmer's book professes to be a complete exposition of the scientific principles of cookery, and holds a high rank in the didactic literature of France. We half suspect that Monsieur Curmer obtained his knowledge of English beef in the same way as did the poor Frenchman, whom the late Mr Mathews, the comedian, so humorously described. Mr Lewis, in his *Physiology of Common Life*, has thus revived the story of the beef-eating son of France: 'A Frenchman was one day blandly remonstrating against the supercilious scorn expressed by Englishmen for the beef of France, which he, for his part, did not find so inferior to that of England. "I have been two times in England," he remarked, "but I nevère find the bif so supérieur to ours. I find it vary conveenient that they bring it you on leetle pieces of stick, for one penny: but I do not find the bif supérieur." On hearing this, the Englishman, red with astonishment, exclaimed, "Good heavens, sir! you have been eating cat's meat."' No, Monsieur Curmer, we are ready to acknowledge the superiority of your cookery, but we have long since made up our minds as to the inferiority of your raw material.

Recipes for Mutton and Lamb

GENERAL OBSERVATIONS ON SHEEP AND LAMBS

Of all wild or domesticated animals, the sheep is, without exception, the most useful to man as a food, and the most necessary to his health and comfort; for it not only supplies him with the lightest and most nutritious of meats, but, in the absence of the cow, its udder yields him milk, cream, and a sound though inferior cheese; while from its fat he obtains light, and from its fleece broadcloth, kerseymere, blankets, gloves, and hose. Its bones when burnt make an animal charcoal – ivory black – to polish his boots, and when powdered, a manure for the cultivation of his wheat; the skin, either split or whole, is made into a mat for his carriage, a housing for his horse, or a lining for his hat, and many other useful purposes besides, being extensively employed in the manufacture of parchment; and finally, when oppressed by care and sorrow, the harmonious strains that carry such soothing contentment to the heart, are elicited from the musical strings, prepared almost exclusively from the intestines of the sheep.

AN EXCELLENT WAY TO COOK A BREAST OF MUTTON

Ingredients – Breast of mutton, 2 onions, salt and pepper to taste, flour, a bunch of savoury herbs, green peas.
Mode – Cut the mutton into pieces about 2 inches square, and let it be tolerably lean; put it into a stewpan, with a little fat or butter, and fry it of a nice brown; then dredge in a little flour, slice the onions, and put it with the herbs in the stewpan; pour in sufficient water just to cover the meat, and simmer the whole gently until the mutton is tender. Take out the meat, strain, and skim off all the fat from the gravy, and put both the meat and gravy back into the stewpan; add about a quart of young green peas, and let them boil gently until done. 2 or 3 slices of bacon added and stewed with the mutton give additional flavour; and, to insure the peas being a beautiful green colour, they may be boiled in water separately, and added to the stew at the moment of serving.
Time – 2½ hours. *Average cost* – 6*d*. per lb.
Seasonable – from June to August. Sufficient for 4 or 5 persons.

Names of Animals Saxon, and of Their Flesh Norman

The names of all our domestic animals are of Saxon origin; but it is curious to observe that Norman names have been given to the different sorts of flesh which these animals yield. How beautifully this illustrates the relative position of Saxon and Norman after the Conquest. The Saxon hind had the charge of tending and feeding the domestic animals, but only that they might appear on the table of his Norman lord. Thus 'ox', 'steer', 'cow', are Saxon, but 'beef' is Norman; 'calf' is Saxon, but 'veal' Norman; 'sheep' is Saxon, but 'mutton' Norman; so it is severally with 'deer' and 'venison', 'swine' and 'pork', 'fowl' and 'pullet'. 'Bacon', the only flesh which, perhaps, ever came within his reach, is the single exception.

HASHED MUTTON

Ingredients – The remains of cold roast shoulder or leg of mutton, 6 whole peppers, 6 whole allspice, a faggot of savoury herbs, ½ head of celery, 1 onion, 2 oz. of butter, flour.
Mode – Cut the meat in nice even slices from the bones, trimming off all superfluous fat and gristle; chop the bones and fragments of the joint, put them into a stewpan with the pepper, spice, herbs, and celery; cover with water, and simmer for 1 hour. Slice and fry the onion of a nice pale-brown colour, dredge in a little flour to make it thick, and add this to the bones, etc. Stew for ¼ hour, strain the gravy, and let it cool; then skim off every particle of fat, and put it, with the meat, into a stewpan. Flavour with ketchup, Harvey's sauce, tomato sauce, or any flavouring that may be preferred, and let the meat gradually warm through, but not boil, or it will harden. To hash meat properly, it should be laid in cold gravy, and only left on the fire just long enough to warm through.
Time – 1½ hour to simmer the gravy. *Average cost* – exclusive of the meat, 4*d*.
Seasonable – at any time.

*

Many persons express a decided aversion to hashed mutton; and, doubtless, this dislike has arisen from the fact that they have unfortunately never been properly served with this dish. If properly done, however, the meat tender (it ought to be as tender as when first roasted), the gravy abundant and well flavoured, and the sippets nicely toasted, and the whole served neatly; then, hashed mutton is by no means to be despised, and is infinitely more wholesome and appetizing than the cold leg or shoulder, of which fathers and husbands, and their bachelor friends, stand in such natural awe.

HODGE-PODGE

Cold meat cookery

Ingredients – About 1 lb. of underdone cold mutton, 2 lettuces, 1 pint of green peas, 5 or 6 green onions, 2 oz. of butter, pepper and salt to taste, ½ teacupful of water.
Mode – Mince the mutton, and cut up the lettuces and onions in slices. Put these in a stewpan, with all the ingredients except the peas, and let these simmer very gently for ¾ hour, keeping them well stirred. Boil the peas separately, mix these with the mutton, and serve very hot.
Time – ¾ hour. Sufficient for 3 or 4 persons.
Seasonable – from the end of May to August.

Recipes for Pork

PORK CHEESE

An excellent Breakfast dish

Ingredients – 2 lb. of cold roast pork, pepper and salt to taste, 1 dessertspoonful of minced parsley, 4 leaves of sage, a very small bunch of savoury herbs, 2 blades of pounded mace, a little nutmeg, ½ teaspoonful of minced lemon-peel; good strong gravy, sufficient to fill the mould.
Mode – Cut, but do not chop, the pork into fine pieces, and allow ¼ lb. of fat to each pound of lean. Season with pepper and salt; pound well the spices, and chop finely the parsley, sage, herbs, and lemon-peel, and mix the whole nicely together. Put it into a mould, fill up with good strong well-flavoured gravy, and bake rather more than one hour. When cold, turn it out of the mould.
Time – Rather more than 1 hour.
Seasonable – from October to March.

PORK PIES

A Warwickshire recipe

Ingredients – For the crust, 5 lb. of lard to 14 lb. of flour, milk, and water. For filling the pies, to every 3 lb. of meat allow 1 oz. of salt, 2¼ oz. of pepper, a small quantity of cayenne, 1 pint of water.

Mode – Rub into the flour a portion of the lard; the remainder put with sufficient milk and water to mix the crust, and boil this gently for ¼ hour. Pour it boiling on the flour, and knead and beat it till perfectly smooth. Now raise the crust in either a round or oval form, cut up the pork into pieces the size of a nut, season it in the above proportion, and press it compactly into the pie, in alternate layers of fat and lean, and pour in a small quantity of water; lay on the lid, cut the edges smoothly round, and pinch them together. Bake in a brick oven, which should be slow, as the meat is very solid. Very frequently, the inexperienced cook finds much difficulty in raising the crust. She should bear in mind that it must not be allowed to get cold, or it will fall immediately: to prevent this, the operation should be performed as near the fire as possible. As considerable dexterity and expertness are necessary to raise the crust with the hand only, a glass bottle or small jar may be placed in the middle of the paste, and the crust moulded on this; but be particular that it is kept warm the whole time.
Sufficient – The proportions for 1 pie are 1 lb. of flour and 3 lb. of meat.
Seasonable – from September to March.

The Flesh of Swine in Hot Climates

It is observed by Monsieur Sonini, that the flesh of swine, in hot climates, is considered unwholesome, and therefore may account for its proscription by the legislators and priests of the East. In Egypt, Syria, and even the southern parts of Greece, although both white and delicate, it is so flabby and surcharged with fat, that it disagrees with the strongest stomachs. Abstinence from it in general was, therefore, indispensable to health under the burning suns of Egypt and Arabia. The Egyptians were permitted to eat it only once a year – on the feast of the moon; and then they sacrificed a number of these animals to that planet. At other seasons, should any one even touch a hog, he was obliged immediately to plunge into the river Nile, as he stood, with his clothes on, in order to purify himself fróm the supposed contamination he had contracted by the touch.

SAUSAGE-MEAT CAKES

Ingredients – To every lb. of lean pork, add ¾ lb. of fat bacon, ¼ oz. of salt, 1 salt-spoonful of pepper, ¼ teaspoonful of grated nutmeg, 1 teaspoonful of minced parsley.
Mode – Remove from the pork all skin, gristle, and bone, and chop it finely with the bacon; add the remaining ingredients, and carefully mix altogether. Pound it well in a mortar, make it into convenient-sized cakes, flour these, and fry them a nice brown for about 10 minutes. This is a very simple method of making sausage-meat, and on trial will prove very good, its great recommendation being, that it is so easily made.
Time – 10 minutes.
Seasonable – from September to March.

The Learned Pig

That the pig is capable of education, is a fact long known to the world; and though, like the ass, naturally stubborn and obstinate, that he is equally amenable with other animals to caresses and kindness, has been shown from very remote time; the best modern evidence of his docility, however, is the instance of the learned pig, first exhibited about a century since, but which has been continued down to our own time by repeated instances of an animal who will put together all the letters or figures that compose the day, month, hour, and date of the exhibition, besides many other unquestioned evidences of memory. The instance already given of breaking a sow into a pointer, till she became more stanch even than the dog itself, though surprising, is far less wonderful than that evidence of education where so generally obtuse an animal may be taught not only to spell, but couple figures and give dates correctly.

Recipes for Veal

VEAL CAKE

A convenient dish for a picnic

Ingredients – A few slices of cold roast veal, a few slices of cold ham, 2 hardboiled eggs, 2 tablespoonfuls of minced parsley, a little pepper, good gravy.
Mode – Cut off all the brown outside from the veal, and cut the eggs into slices. Procure a pretty mould; lay veal, ham, eggs, and parsley in layers, with a little pepper between each, and when the mould is full, get some strong stock, and fill up the shape. Bake for ½ hour, and when cold, turn it out.
Time – ½ hour. *Seasonable* – at any time.

MINCED VEAL AND MACARONI

A pretty side or corner dish

Ingredients – ¾ lb. of minced cold roast veal, 3 oz. of ham, 1 tablespoonful of gravy, pepper and salt to taste, ¼ teaspoonful of grated nutmeg, ¼ lb. of bread crumbs, ¼ lb. of macaroni, 1 or 2 eggs to bind, a small piece of butter.
Mode – Cut some nice slices from a cold fillet of veal, trim off the brown outside, and mince the meat finely with the above proportion of ham: should the meat be very dry, add a spoonful of good gravy. Season highly

with pepper and salt, add the grated nutmeg and bread crumbs, and mix these ingredients with 1 or 2 eggs well beaten, which should bind the mixture and make it like forcemeat. In the meantime, boil the macaroni in salt and water, and drain it; butter a mould, put some of the macaroni at the bottom and sides of it, in whatever form is liked; mix the remainder with the forcemeat, fill the mould up to the top, put a plate or small dish on it, and steam for ½ hour. Turn it out carefully, and serve with good gravy poured round, but not over, the meat.

Time – ½ hour.

Average cost – exclusive of the cold meat, 10*d*.

Seasonable – from March to October.

Note – To make a variety, boil some carrots and turnips separately in a little salt and water; when done, cut them into pieces about ⅛ inch in thickness; butter an oval mould, and place these in it, in white and red stripes alternately, at the bottom and sides. Proceed as in the foregoing recipe, and be very careful in turning it out of the mould.

Recipes for Poultry and Rabbits

STEWED DUCK AND PEAS

Cold meat cookery

Ingredients – The remains of cold roast duck, 2 oz. of butter, 3 or 4 slices of lean ham or bacon, 1 tablespoonful of flour, 2 pints of thin gravy, 1, or a small bunch of green onions, 3 sprigs of parsley, 3 cloves, 1 pint of young green peas, cayenne and salt to taste, 1 teaspoonful of pounded sugar.

Mode – Put the butter into a stewpan; cut up the duck into joints, lay them in with the slices of lean ham or bacon; make it brown, then dredge in a tablespoonful of flour, and stir this well in before adding the gravy. Put in the onion, parsley, cloves, and gravy, and when it has simmered for ¼ hour, add a pint of young green peas, and stew gently for about ½ hour. Season with cayenne, salt, and sugar; take out the duck, place it round the dish, and the peas in the middle.

Time – ¾ hour.

Average cost – exclusive of the cold duck, 1*s*.

Seasonable – from June to August.

Space for Fowls

We are no advocates for converting the domestic fowl into a cage-bird. We have known amateur fowl-keepers –

worthy souls, who would butter the very barley they gave their pets, if they thought they would the more enjoy it – coop up a male bird and three or four hens in an ordinary egg-chest placed on its side, and with the front closely barred with iron hooping! This system will not do. Every animal, from man himself to the guinea-pig, must have what is vulgarly, but truly, known as 'elbow-room'; and it must be self-evident how emphatically this rule applies to winged animals. It may be urged, in the case of domestic fowls, that from constant disuse, and from clipping and plucking, and other sorts of maltreatment, their wings can hardly be regarded as instruments of flight; we maintain, however, that you may pluck a fowl's wing-joints as bare as a pumpkin, but you will not erase from his memory that he is a fowl, and that his proper sphere is the open air. If he likewise reflects that he is an ill-used fowl – a prison-bird – he will then come to the conclusion, that there is not the least use, under such circumstances, for his existence; and you must admit that the decision is only logical and natural.

FRICASSEED FOWL

Cold meat cookery

Ingredients – The remains of cold roast fowl, 1 strip of lemon-peel, 1 blade of pounded mace, 1 bunch of savoury herbs, 1 onion, pepper and salt to taste, 1 pint of water, 1 teaspoonful of flour, ¼ pint of cream, the yolks of 2 eggs. *Mode* – Carve the fowls into nice joints; make gravy of the trimmings and legs, by stewing them with the lemon-peel, mace, herbs, onion, seasoning, and water, until reduced

to ½ pint; then strain, and put in the fowl. Warm it through, and thicken with a teaspoonful of flour; stir the yolks of the eggs into the cream; add these to the sauce, let it get thoroughly hot, but do not allow it to boil, or it will curdle.
Time – 1 hour to make the gravy, ¼ hour to warm the fowl.
Average cost – exclusive of the cold chicken, 8*d*.
Seasonable – at any time.

The Best Way to Fatten Fowls

The barn-door fowl is in itself a complete refutation of the cramming and dungeon policy of feeding practised by some. This fowl, which has the common run of the farm-yard, living on dairy-scraps and offal from the stable, begins to grow fat at threshing-time. He has his fill of the finest corn; he has his fill of fresh air and natural exercise, and at last he comes smoking to the table – a dish for the gods. In the matter of unnaturally stuffing and confining fowls, Mowbray is exactly of our opinion. He says: 'The London chicken-butchers, as they are termed, are said to be, of all others, the most expeditious and dexterous feeders, putting up a coop of fowls, and making them thoroughly fat within the space of a fortnight, using much grease, and that perhaps not of the most delicate kind, in the food. In this way I have no boasts to make, having always found it necessary to allow a considerable number of weeks for the purpose of making fowls fat in coops. In the common way this business is often badly managed, fowls being huddled together in a small coop, tearing each other to pieces, instead of enjoying that repose which alone can insure, the wished-for object – irregularly fed and cleaned, until they become so stenched and poisoned in their own excrement, that their flesh actually smells and tastes when smoking upon the table.' Sussex produces the fattest and largest poultry of any county in England, and the fatting process there most common is to give them a gruel made of pot-liquor and bruised oats, with which are mixed hog's grease, sugar, and milk. The fowls are kept very warm, and crammed morning and night. They are put into the coop, and kept there two or three days before the cramming begins, and then it is continued for a fortnight, and the birds are sent to market.

HASHED FOWL, INDIAN FASHION
An Entrée

Ingredients – The remains of cold roast fowl, 3 or 4 sliced onions, 1 apple, 2 oz. of butter, pounded mace, pepper and salt to taste, 1 tablespoonful of curry-powder, 2 tablespoonfuls of vinegar, 1 tablespoonful of flour, 1 teaspoonful of pounded sugar, 1 pint of gravy.
Mode – Cut the onions into slices, mince the apple, and fry these in the butter; add pounded mace, pepper, salt, curry-powder, vinegar, flour, and sugar in the above proportions; when the onion is brown, put it the gravy, which should be previously made from the bones and trimmings of the fowls, and stew for ¾ hour; add the fowl cut into nice-sized joints, let it warm through, and when quite tender, serve. The dish should be garnished with an edging of boiled rice.

Time – 1 hour. *Average cost* – exclusive of the fowl, 8*d*. *Seasonable* – at any time.

LARK PIE
An Entrée

Ingredients – A few thin slices of beef, the same of bacon, 9 larks, flour; for stuffing, 1 teacupful of bread crumbs, ½ teaspoonful of minced lemon-peel, 1 teaspoonful of minced parsley, 1 egg, salt and pepper to taste, 1 teaspoonful of chopped shalot, ½ pint of weak stock or water, puff-paste.

Mode – Make a stuffing of bread crumbs, minced lemon-peel, parsley, and the yolk of an egg, all of which should be well mixed together; roll the larks in flour, and stuff them. Line the bottom of a pie-dish with a few slices of beef and bacon; over these place the larks, and season with salt, pepper, minced parsley, and chopped shalot, in the above proportion. Pour in the stock or water, cover with crust, and bake for an hour in a moderate oven. During the time the pie is baking, shake it 2 or 3 times, to assist in thickening the gravy, and serve very hot.

Time – 1 hour. *Average cost* – 1*s*. 6*d*. a dozen.

Sufficient for 5 or 6 persons.

Seasonable – In full season in November.

FRIED RABBIT

Ingredients – 1 rabbit, flour, dripping, 1 oz. of butter, 1 teaspoonful of minced shalot, 2 tablespoonfuls of mushroom ketchup.

Mode – Cut the rabbit into neat joints, and flour them well; make the dripping boiling in a frying-pan, put in the rabbit, and fry it a nice brown. Have ready a very hot dish, put in the butter, shalot, and ketchup; arrange the rabbit pyramidically on this, and serve as quickly as possible.
Time – 10 minutes. *Average cost* – from 1*s*. to 1*s*. 6*d*. each.
Seasonable – from September to February. Sufficient for 4 or 5 persons.
Note – The rabbit may be brushed over with egg, and sprinkled with bread crumbs, and fried as above. When cooked in this manner, make a gravy in the pan and pour it round, but not over, the pieces of rabbit.

RABBIT PIE

Ingredients – 1 rabbit, a few slices of ham, salt and white pepper to taste, 2 blades of pounded mace, ½ teaspoonful of grated nutmeg, a few forcemeat balls, 3 hard-boiled eggs, ½ pint of gravy, puff crust.
Mode – Cut up the rabbit (which should be young), remove the breastbone, and bone the legs. Put the rabbit, slices of ham, forcemeat balls, and hard eggs, by turns, in layers, and season each layer with pepper, salt, pounded mace, and grated nutmeg. Pour in about ½ pint of water, cover with crust, and bake in a well-heated oven for about 1½ hour. Should the crust acquire too much colour, place a piece of paper over it to prevent its burning. When done, pour in at the top, by means of the hole in the middle of the crust, a little good gravy,

which may be made of the breast and leg-bones of the rabbit and 2 or 3 shank-bones, flavoured with onion, herbs, and spices.

Time – 1½ hour. *Average cost* – from 1*s*. to 1*s*. 6*d*. each. Sufficient for 5 or 6 persons.

Seasonable – from September to February.

Note – The liver of the rabbit may be boiled, minced, and mixed with the forcemeat balls, when the flavour is liked.

Recipes for Game

JUGGED HARE

Ingredients – 1 hare, a bunch of sweet herbs, 2 onions, each stuck with 3 cloves, 6 whole allspice, ½ teaspoonful of black pepper, a strip of lemon-peel, thickening of butter and flour, 2 tablespoonfuls of mushroom ketchup, ¼ pint of port wine.

Mode – Wash the hare nicely, cut it up into joints (not too large), and flour and brown them; then put them into a stewpan with the herbs, onions, cloves, allspice, pepper, and lemon-peel; cover with hot water, and when it boils, carefully remove all the scum, and let it simmer gently till tender, which will be in about 1¾ hour, or longer, should the hare be very old. Take out the pieces of hare, thicken the gravy with flour and butter, add the ketchup and port wine, let it boil for about 10 minutes, strain it through a sieve over the hare, and serve. A few fried forcemeat balls should be added at the moment of serving, or instead of frying them, they may be stewed in the gravy, about 10 minutes before the hare is wanted for table. Do not omit to serve red-currant jelly with it.

Time – Altogether 2 hours. *Average cost* – 5*s*. 6*d*.

Sufficient for 7 or 8 persons.

Seasonable – from September to the end of February.

Note – Should there be any left, rewarm it the next day by putting the hare, etc. into a covered jar, and placing this jar in a saucepan of boiling water: this method prevents a great deal of waste.

POTTED PARTRIDGE

Ingredients – Partridges; seasoning to taste of mace, allspice, white pepper, and salt; butter, coarse paste.
Mode – Pluck and draw the birds, and wipe them inside with a damp cloth. Pound well some mace, allspice, white pepper, and salt; mix together, and rub every part of the partridges with this. Pack the birds as closely as possible in a baking-pan, with plenty of butter over them, and cover with a coarse flour and water crust. Tie a paper over this, and bake for rather more than 1½ hour; let the birds get cold, then cut them into pieces for keeping, pack them closely into a large potting-pot, and cover with clarified butter. This should be kept in a cool dry place. The butter used for potted things will answer for basting, or for paste for meat pies.
Time – 1½ hour.
Seasonable – from the 1st of September to the beginning of February.

VENISON

This is the name given to the flesh of some kinds of deer, and is esteemed as very delicious. Different species of deer are found in warm as well as cold climates, and are in several instances invaluable to man. This is especially the case with the Laplander, whose reindeer constitutes a large proportion of his wealth. There

> The reindeer unharness'd in freedom can play,
> And safely o'er Odin's steep precipice stray,
> Whilst the wolf to the forest recesses may fly,
> And howl to the moon as she glides through the sky.

In that country it is the substitute for the horse, the cow, the goat, and the sheep. From its milk is produced cheese; from its skin, clothing; from its tendons, bowstrings and thread; from its horns, glue; from its bones, spoons; and its flesh furnishes food. In England we have the stag, an animal of great beauty, and much admired. He is a native of many parts of Europe, and is supposed to have been originally introduced into this country from France. About a century back he was to be found wild in some of the rough and mountainous parts of Wales, as well as in the forests of Exmoor, in Devonshire, and the woods on the banks of the Tamar. In the middle ages the deer formed food for the not over abstemious monks, as represented by Friar Tuck's larder, in the admirable fiction of *Ivanhoe*; and at a later period it was a deer-stealing adventure that drove the 'ingenious' William Shakespeare to London, to become a common player, and the greatest dramatist that ever lived.

STEWED VENISON

Ingredients – A shoulder of venison, a few slices of mutton fat, 2 glasses of port wine, pepper and allspice to taste, 1½ pint of weak stock or gravy, ½ teaspoonful of whole pepper, ½ teaspoonful of whole allspice.

Mode – Hang the venison till tender; take out the bone, flatten the meat with a rolling-pin, and place over it a few slices of mutton fat, which have been previously soaked for 2 or 3 hours in port wine; sprinkle these with a little fine allspice and pepper, roll the meat up, and bind and tie it securely. Put it into a stewpan with the bone and the above proportion of weak stock or gravy, whole allspice, black pepper, and port wine; cover the lid down closely, and simmer, very gently, from 3½ to 4 hours. When quite tender, take off the tape, and dish the meat; strain the gravy over it, and send it to table with red-currant jelly. Unless the joint is very fat, the above is the best mode of cooking it.
Time – 3½ to 4 hours.
Average cost – 1*s*. 4*d*. to 1*s*. 6*d*. per lb.
Sufficient for 10 or 12 persons.
Seasonable – Buck venison, from June to Michaelmas; doe venison, from November to the end of January.

Recipes for Vegetables

ASPARAGUS PUDDING

A delicious Dish, to be served with the Second Course

Ingredients – ½ pint of asparagus peas, 4 eggs, 2 tablespoonfuls of flour, 1 tablespoonful of very finely minced ham, 1 oz. of butter, pepper and salt to taste, milk.
Mode – Cut up the nice green tender parts of asparagus, about the size of peas; put them into a basin with the eggs, which should be well beaten, and the flour, ham, butter, pepper, and salt. Mix all these ingredients well together, and moisten with sufficient milk to make the pudding of the consistency of thick batter; put it into a pint buttered mould, tie it down tightly with a floured cloth, place it in boiling water, and let it boil for 2 hours; turn it out of the mould on to a hot dish, and pour plain melted butter round, but not over, the pudding. Green peas pudding may be made in exactly the same manner, substituting peas for the asparagus.
Time – 2 hours. *Average cost* – 1s. 6*d*. per pint.
Seasonable – in May, June, and July.

BOILED BRUSSELS SPROUTS

Ingredients – To each ½ gallon of water allow 1 heaped tablespoonful of salt; a very small piece of soda.

Mode – Clean the sprouts from insects, nicely wash them, and pick off any dead or discoloured leaves from the outsides; put them into a saucepan of boiling water, with salt and soda in the above proportion; keep the pan uncovered, and let them boil quickly over a brisk fire until tender; drain, dish, and serve with a tureen of melted butter, or with a maître d'hôtel sauce poured over them. Another mode of serving is, when they are dished, to stir in about 1½ oz. of butter and a seasoning of pepper and salt. They must, however, be sent to table very quickly, as, being so very small, this vegetable soon cools. Where the cook is very expeditious, this vegetable, when cooked, may be arranged on the dish in the form of a pineapple, and, so served, has a very pretty appearance.

Time – From 9 to 12 minutes after the water boils.

Average cost – 1*s*. 4*d*. per peck. *Seasonable* – from November to March.

Sufficient – Allow between 40 and 50 for 5 or 6 persons.

HORSERADISH

This root, scraped, is always served with hot roast beef, and is used for garnishing many kinds of boiled fish. Let the horseradish remain in cold water for an hour; wash it well, and with a sharp knife scrape it into very thin shreds, commencing from the thick end of the root. Arrange some of it lightly in a small glass dish, and the remainder use for garnishing the joint: it should be placed in tufts round the border of the dish, with 1 or 2 bunches on the meat.

Average cost – 2*d*. per stick. *Seasonable* – from October to June.

The Horseradish

This belongs to the tribe *Alyssidae*, and is highly stimulant and exciting to the stomach. It has been recommended in chronic rheumatism, palsy, dropsical complaints, and in cases of enfeebled digestion. Its principal use, however, is as a condiment to promote appetite and excite the digestive organs. The horseradish contains sulphur to the extent of thirty per cent, in the number of its elements; and it is to the presence of this quality that the metal vessels in which the radish is sometimes distilled, are turned into a black colour. It is one of the most powerful excitants and antiscorbutics we have, and forms the basis of several medical preparations, in the form of wines, tinctures, and syrups.

SUMMER SALAD

Ingredients – 3 lettuces, 2 handfuls of mustard-and-cress, 10 young radishes, a few slices of cucumber.
Mode – Let the herbs be as fresh as possible for a salad, and, if at all stale or dead-looking, let them lie in water for an hour or two, which will very much refresh them. Wash and carefully pick them over, remove any decayed or worm-eaten leaves, and drain them thoroughly by swinging them gently in a clean cloth. With a silver knife, cut the lettuces into small pieces, and the radishes and cucumbers into thin slices; arrange all these ingredients lightly on a dish, with the mustard-and-cress, and

pour under, but not over the salad [the salad dressing (p. 48)] and do not stir it up until it is to be eaten. It may be garnished with hard-boiled eggs, cut in slices, sliced cucumbers, nasturtiums, cut vegetable-flowers, and many other things that taste will always suggest to make a pretty and elegant dish. In making a good salad, care must be taken to have the herbs freshly gathered, and thoroughly drained before the sauce is added to them, or it will be watery and thin. Young spring onions, cut small, are by many persons considered an improvement to salads; but, before these are added, the cook should always consult the taste of her employer. Slices of cold meat or poultry added to a salad make a convenient and quickly-made summer luncheon-dish; or cold fish, flaked, will also be found exceedingly nice, mixed with it.

Average cost – 9*d*. for a salad for 5 or 6 persons; but more expensive when the herbs are forced.
Sufficient for 5 or 6 persons.
Seasonable – from May to September.

Cucumbers

The cucumber is refreshing, but neither nutritious nor digestible, and should be excluded from the regimen of the delicate. There are various modes of preparing cucumbers. When gathered young, they are called gherkins: these, pickled, are much used in seasonings.

Recipes for Puddings and Pastry

AUNT NELLY'S PUDDING

Ingredients – ½ lb. of flour, ½ lb. of treacle, ½ lb. of suet, the rind and juice of 1 lemon, a few strips of candied lemon-peel, 3 tablespoonfuls of cream, 2 eggs.
Mode – Chop the suet finely; mix with it the flour, treacle, lemon-peel minced, and candied lemon-peel; add the cream, lemon-juice, and 2 well-beaten eggs; beat the pudding well, put it into a buttered basin, tie it down with a cloth, and boil from 3½ to 4 hours.
Time – 3½ to 4 hours. *Average cost* – 1s. 2*d.*
Sufficient for 5 or 6 persons.
Seasonable – at any time, but more suitable for a winter pudding.

APPLE SNOWBALLS

Ingredients – 2 teacupfuls of rice, apples, moist sugar, cloves.
Mode – Boil the rice in milk until three-parts done; then strain it off, and pare and core the apples without dividing them. Put a small quantity of sugar and a clove into each apple, put the rice round them, and tie each ball separately in a cloth. Boil until the apples are tender; then take them up, remove the cloths, and serve.

Time – ½ hour to boil the rice separately; ½ to 1 hour with the apple.
Seasonable – from August to March.

A BACHELOR'S PUDDING

Ingredients – 4 oz. of grated bread, 4 oz. of currants, 4 oz. of apples, 2 oz. of sugar, 3 eggs, a few drops of essence of lemon, a little grated nutmeg.
Mode – Pare, core, and mince the apples very finely, sufficient, when minced, to make 4 oz.; add to these the currants, which should be well washed, the grated bread, and sugar; whisk the eggs, beat these up with the remaining ingredients, and, when all is thoroughly mixed, put the pudding into a buttered basin, tie it down with a cloth, and boil for 3 hours.
Time – 3 hours. *Average cost* – 9*d.*
Sufficient for 4 or 5 persons. *Seasonable* – from August to March.

FIG PUDDING

Ingredients – 2 lb. of figs, 1 lb. of suet, ½ lb. of flour, ½ lb. of bread crumbs, 2 eggs, milk.
Mode – Cut the figs into small pieces, grate the bread finely, and chop the suet very small; mix these well together, add the flour, the eggs, which should be well beaten, and sufficient milk to form the whole into a stiff paste; butter a mould or basin, press the pudding into it very closely, tie it down with a cloth, and boil for 3

hours, or rather longer; turn it out of the mould, and serve with melted butter, wine-sauce, or cream.
Time – 3 hours or longer. *Average cost* – 2*s*. Sufficient for 7 or 8 persons.
Seasonable – Suitable for a winter pudding.

MONDAY'S PUDDING

Ingredients – The remains of cold plum-pudding, brandy, custard made with 5 eggs to every pint of milk.
Mode – Cut the remains of a good cold plum-pudding into finger-pieces, soak them in a little brandy, and lay them cross-barred in a mould until full. Make a custard with the above proportion of milk and eggs, flavouring it with nutmeg or lemon-rind; fill up the mould with it; tie it down with a cloth, and boil or steam it for an hour. Serve with a little of the custard poured over, to which has been added a tablespoonful of brandy.
Time – 1 hour.
Average cost – exclusive of the pudding, 6*d*.
Sufficient for 5 or 6 persons.
Seasonable – at any time.

Recipes for Creams and Sweet Dishes

BAKED-APPLE CUSTARD

Ingredients – 1 dozen large apples, moist sugar to taste, 1 small teacupful of cold water, the grated rind of one lemon, 1 pint of milk, 4 eggs, 2 oz. of loaf sugar.
Mode – Peel, cut, and core the apples; put them into a lined saucepan with the cold water, and as they heat, bruise them to a pulp; sweeten with moist sugar, and add the grated lemon-rind. When cold, put the fruit at the bottom of a pie-dish, and pour over it a custard, made with the above proportion of milk, eggs, and sugar; grate a little nutmeg over the top, place the dish in a moderate oven, and bake from 25 to 35 minutes. The above proportions will make rather a large dish.
Time – 25 to 35 minutes. *Average cost* – 1*s*. 4*d*.
Sufficient for 6 or 7 persons. *Seasonable* – from July to March.

ARROWROOT BLANCMANGE

An inexpensive supper dish

Ingredients – 4 heaped tablespoonfuls of arrowroot, 1½ pint of milk, 3 laurel-leaves or the rind of ½ lemon, sugar to taste.
Mode – Mix to a smooth batter the arrowroot with ½

pint of the milk; put the other pint on the fire, with laurel-leaves or lemon-peel, whichever may be preferred, and let the milk steep until it is well flavoured. Then strain the milk, and add it, boiling, to the mixed arrow-root; sweeten it with sifted sugar, and let it boil, stirring it all the time, till it thickens sufficiently to come from the saucepan. Grease a mould with pure salad-oil, pour in the blancmange, and when quite set, turn it out on a dish, and pour round it a compôte of any kind of fruit, or garnish it with jam. A tablespoonful of brandy, stirred in just before the blancmange is moulded, very much improves the flavour of this sweet dish.
Time – Altogether, ½ hour. *Average cost* – 6*d*. without the garnishing.
Sufficient for 4 or 5 persons.
Seasonable – at any time.

GINGER CREAM

Ingredients – The yolks of 4 eggs, 1 pint of cream, 3 oz. of preserved ginger, 2 dessertspoonfuls of syrup, sifted sugar to taste, 1 oz. of isinglass.
Mode – Slice the ginger finely; put it into a basin with the syrup, the well-beaten yolks of eggs, and the cream; mix these ingredients well together, and stir them over the fire for about 10 minutes, or until the mixture thickens; then take it off the fire, whisk till nearly cold, sweeten to taste, add the isinglass, which should be melted and strained, and serve the cream in a glass dish. It may be garnished with slices of preserved ginger or candied citron.

Time – About 10 minutes to stir the cream over the fire. *Average cost* – with cream at 1*s*. per pint, 3*s*. 6*d*. Sufficient for a good-sized dish. *Seasonable* – at any time.

Preserved ginger comes to us from the West Indies. It is made by scalding the roots when they are green and full of sap, then peeling them in cold water, and putting them into jars, with a rich syrup; in which state we receive them. It should be chosen of a bright-yellow colour, with a little transparency: what is dark-coloured, fibrous, and stringy, is not good. Ginger roots, fit for preserving, and in size equal to West Indian, have been produced in the Royal Agricultural Garden in Edinburgh.

TO MAKE SYLLABUB

Ingredients – 1 pint of sherry or white wine, ½ grated nutmeg, sugar to taste, 1½ pint of milk.
Mode – Put the wine into a bowl, with the grated nutmeg and plenty of pounded sugar, and milk into it the above proportion of milk frothed up. Clouted cream may be laid on the top, with pounded cinnamon or nutmeg and sugar; and a little brandy may be added to the wine before the milk is put in. In some counties, cider is substituted for the wine: when this is used, brandy must always be added. Warm milk may be poured on from a spouted jug or teapot; but it must be held very high.
Average cost – 2*s*. Sufficient for 5 or 6 persons. *Seasonable* – at any time.

TIPSY CAKE

Ingredients – 1 moulded sponge- or Savoy-cake, sufficient sweet wine or sherry to soak it, 6 tablespoonfuls of brandy, 2 oz. of sweet almonds, 1 pint of rich custard.
Mode – Procure a cake that is three or four days old – either sponge, Savoy, or rice answering for the purpose of a tipsy cake. Cut the bottom of the cake level, to make it stand firm in the dish; make a small hole in the centre, and pour in and over the cake sufficient sweet wine or sherry, mixed with the above proportion of brandy, to soak it nicely. When the cake is well soaked, blanch and cut the almonds into strips, stick them all over the cake, and pour round it a good custard, allowing 8 eggs to the pint of milk. The cakes are sometimes crumbled and soaked, and a whipped cream heaped over them, the same as for trifles.
Time – About 2 hours to soak the cake. *Average cost* – 4*s*. 6*d*.
Sufficient for 1 dish. *Seasonable* – at any time.

Recipes for Confectionary, Ices and Dessert Dishes

DESSERT DISHES

With moderns the dessert is not so profuse, nor does it hold the same relationship to the dinner that it held with the ancients – the Romans more especially. On ivory tables they would spread hundreds of different kinds of raw, cooked, and preserved fruits, tarts and cakes, as substitutes for the more substantial comestibles with which the guests were satiated. However, as late as the reigns of our two last Georges, fabulous sums were often expended upon fanciful desserts. The dessert certainly repays, in its general effect, the expenditure upon it of much pains; and it may be said, that if there be any poetry at all in meals, or the process of feeding, there is poetry in the dessert, the materials for which should be selected with taste, and, of course, must depend, in a great measure, upon the season. Pines, melons, grapes, peaches, nectarines, plums, strawberries, apples, pears, oranges, almonds, raisins, figs, walnuts, filberts, medlars, cherries, etc. etc., all kinds of dried fruits, and choice and delicately-flavoured cakes and biscuits, make up the dessert, together with the most costly and recherché wines. The shape of the dishes varies at different periods, the prevailing fashion at present being oval and circular dishes on stems. The patterns and colours are also subject to changes of fashion; some persons selecting china, chaste in pattern and colour; others, elegantly-shaped glass dishes on stems, with gilt edges. The beauty of the dessert services at the tables of the wealthy tends to enhance the splendour of the plate. The general mode of putting a dessert on table, now the elegant tazzas are fashionable, is, to place them down the middle of the table, a tall and short dish alternately; the fresh fruits being arranged on the tall dishes, and dried fruits, bonbons, etc., on small round or oval glass plates. The garnishing needs especial attention, as the contrast of the brilliant-coloured fruits with nicely-arranged foliage is very charming. The garnish par excellence for dessert is the ice-plant; its crystallized dewdrops producing a marvellous effect in the height of summer, giving a most inviting sense of coolness to the fruit it encircles. The double-edged mallow, strawberry, and vine leaves have a pleasing effect; and for winter desserts, the bay, cuba, and laurel are sometimes used. In town, the expense and difficulty of obtaining natural foliage is great, but paper and composite leaves are to be purchased at an almost nominal price. Mixed fruits of the larger sort are now frequently served on one dish. This mode admits of the display of much taste in the arrangement of the fruit: for instance, a pine in the centre of the dish, surrounded with large plums of various sorts and colours, mixed with pears, rosy-cheeked apples, all arranged with a due regard to colour, have a very good effect. Again, apples and pears look well mingled with plums and grapes, hanging from the border of the dish in a négligé sort of manner, with a large bunch of the same fruit lying on the top of the apples. A dessert would not now be considered complete without candied and preserved fruits and confections. The candied fruits may be purchased at a less cost than they can be manufactured at home. They are preserved abroad in most ornamental and elegant forms. And since, from the facilities of travel, we have become so familiar with the tables of the French, chocolate in different forms is indispensable to our desserts.

ICES

Ices are composed, it is scarcely necessary to say, of congealed cream or water, combined sometimes with liqueurs or other flavouring ingredients, or more generally with the juices of fruits. At desserts, or at some evening parties, ices are scarcely to be dispensed with. The principal utensils required for making ice-creams are ice-tubs, freezing-pots, spaddles, and a cellaret. The tub must be large enough to contain about a bushel of ice, pounded small, when brought out of the ice-house, and mixed very carefully with either salt, nitre, or soda. The freezing-pot is best made of pewter. If it be of tin, as is sometimes the case, the congelation goes on too rapidly in it for the thorough intermingling of its contents, on which the excellence of the ice greatly depends. The spaddle is generally made of copper, kept bright and clean. The cellaret is a tin vessel, in which ices are kept for a short time from dissolving. The method to be pursued in the freezing process must be attended to. When the ice-tub is prepared with fresh-pounded ice and salt, the freezing-pot is put into it up to its cover. The articles to be congealed are then poured into it and covered over; but to prevent the ingredients from separating and the heaviest of them from falling to the bottom of the mould, it is requisite to turn the freezing-pot round and round by the handle, so as to keep its contents moving until the congelation commences. As soon as this is perceived (the cover of the pot being occasionally taken off for the purpose of noticing when freezing takes place), the cover is immediately closed over it, ice is put upon it, and it is left in this state till it is served. The use of the spaddle is to stir up and remove from the sides of the freezing pot the cream, which in the shaking may have washed against it, and by stirring it in with the rest, to prevent waste of it occurring. Any negligence in stirring the contents of the freezing-pot before congelation takes place, will destroy the whole: either the sugar sinks to the bottom and leaves the ice insufficiently sweetened, or lumps are formed, which disfigure and discolour it.

The aged, the delicate, and children should abstain from ices or iced beverages; even the strong and healthy should partake of them in moderation. They should be taken immediately after the repast, or some hours after, because the taking these substances during the process of digestion is apt to provoke indisposition. It is necessary, then, that this function should have scarcely commenced, or that it should be completely finished, before partaking of ices. It is also necessary to abstain from them when persons are very warm, or immediately after taking violent exercise, as in some cases they have produced illnesses which have ended fatally.

(Do ladies know to whom they are indebted for the introduction of ices, which all the fair sex are passionately fond of? – To Catherine de' Medici. Will not this fact cover a multitude of sins committed by the instigator of St Bartholomew?)

ICED ORANGES

Ingredients – Oranges; to every lb. of pounded loaf sugar allow the whites of 2 eggs.
Mode – Whisk the whites of the eggs well, stir in the sugar, and beat this mixture for ¼ hour. Skin the oranges, remove as much of the white pith as possible without injuring the pulp of the fruit; pass a thread through the centre of each orange, dip them into the sugar, and tie them to a stick. Place this stick across the oven, and let the oranges remain until dry, when they will have the appearance of balls of ice. They make a pretty dessert or supper dish. Care must be taken not to have the oven too fierce, or the oranges would scorch and acquire a brown colour, which would entirely spoil their appearance.
Time – From ½ to 1 hour to dry in a moderate oven.
Average cost – 1½*d.* each.
Sufficient – ½ lb. of sugar to ice 12 oranges.
Seasonable – from November to May.

Orange and Cloves

It appears to have been the custom formerly, in England, to make new year's presents with oranges stuck full with cloves. We read in one of Ben Jonson's pieces – the *Christmas Masque*, – 'He has an orange and rosemary, but not a clove to stick in it.'

PINEAPPLE CHIPS

Ingredients – Pineapples; sugar to taste.
Mode – Pare and slice the fruit thinly, put it on dishes, and strew over it plenty of pounded sugar. Keep it in a hot closet, or very slow oven, 8 or 10 days, and turn the fruit every day until dry; then put the pieces of pine on tins, and place them in a quick oven for 10 minutes. Let them cool, and store them away in dry boxes, with paper between each layer.
Time – 8 to 10 days.
Seasonable – Foreign pines, in July and August.

TO MAKE EVERTON TOFFEE

Ingredients – 1 lb. of powdered loaf sugar, 1 teacupful of water, ¼ lb. of butter, 6 drops of essence of lemon.
Mode – Put the water and sugar into a brass pan, and beat the butter to a cream. When the sugar is dissolved, add the butter, and keep stirring the mixture over the fire until it sets, when a little is poured on to a buttered dish; and just before the toffee is done, add the essence of lemon. Butter a dish or tin, pour on it the mixture, and when cool, it will easily separate from the dish. Butter-Scotch, an excellent thing for coughs, is made with brown, instead of white sugar, omitting the water, and flavoured with ½ oz. of powdered ginger. It is made in the same manner as toffee.
Time – 18 to 35 minutes.
Average cost – 10*d*.
Sufficient to make a lb. of toffee.

Recipes for Milk, Butter, Cheese and Eggs

Milk is one of the most complete of all articles of food: that is to say, it contains a very large number of the elements which enter into the composition of the human body. It 'disagrees' with fat, heavy, languid people, of slow circulation; and, at first, with many people of sedentary habits, and stomachs weakened by stimulants of different kinds. But, if exercise can be taken and a little patience shown, while the system accommodates itself to a new regimen, this bland and soothing article of diet is excellent for the majority of thin, nervous people; especially for those who have suffered much from emotional disturbances, or have relaxed their stomachs by too much tea or coffee, taken too hot. Milk is, in fact, a nutrient and a sedative at once. Stomachs, however, have their idiosyncrasies, and it sometimes proves an unwelcome and ill-digested article of food. As milk, when good, contains a good deal of respiratory material (fat) – material which must either be burnt off, or derange the liver, and be rejected in other ways, it may disagree because the lungs are not sufficiently used in the open air. But it is very probable that there are really 'constitutions' which cannot take to it; and they should not be forced.

CURDS AND WHEY

Ingredients – A very small piece of rennet, ½ gallon of milk. *Mode* – Procure from the butcher's a small piece of rennet, which is the stomach of the calf, taken as soon as it is killed, scoured, and well rubbed with salt, and stretched on sticks to dry. Pour some boiling water on the rennet, and let it remain for 6 hours; then use the liquor to turn the milk. The milk should be warm and fresh from the cow: if allowed to cool, it must be heated till it is of a degree quite equal to new milk; but do not let it be too hot. About a tablespoonful or rather more, would be sufficient to turn the above proportion of milk into curds and whey; and whilst the milk is turning, let it be kept in rather a warm place. *Time* – From 2 to 3 hours to turn the milk. *Seasonable* – at any time.

STILTON CHEESE

Stilton cheese, or British Parmesan, as it is sometimes called, is generally preferred to all other cheeses by those whose authority few will dispute. Those made in May or June are usually served at Christmas; or, to be in prime order, should be kept from 10 to 12 months, or even longer. An artificial ripeness in Stilton cheese is sometimes produced by inserting a small piece of decayed Cheshire into an aperture at the top. From 3 weeks to a month is sufficient time to ripen the cheese. An additional flavour may also be obtained by scooping out a piece from the top, and pouring therein port, sherry, Madeira, or old ale, and letting the cheese absorb these for 2 or 3 weeks. But that cheese is the finest which is ripened without any artificial aid, is the opinion of those who are judges in these matters. In serving a Stilton cheese, the top of it should be cut off to form a lid, and a napkin or piece of white paper, with a frill at the top, pinned round. When the cheese goes from table, the lid should be replaced.

Cheese

It is well known that some persons like cheese in a state of decay, and even 'alive'. There is no accounting for tastes, and it may be hard to show why mould, which is vegetation, should not be eaten as well as salad, or maggots as well as eels. But, generally speaking, decomposing bodies are not wholesome eating, and the line must be drawn somewhere.

Smoking Cheeses

The Romans smoked their cheeses, to give them a sharp taste. They possessed public places expressly for this use, and subject to police regulations which no one could evade.

A celebrated gourmand remarked that a dinner without cheese is like a woman with one eye.

BRILLAT-SAVARIN'S FONDUE

An excellent recipe

Ingredients – Eggs, cheese, butter, pepper and salt.
Mode – Take the same number of eggs as there are guests; weigh the eggs in the shell, allow a third of their weight

in Gruyère cheese, and a piece of butter one-sixth of the weight of the cheese. Break the eggs into a basin, beat them well; add the cheese, which should be grated, and the butter, which should be broken into small pieces. Stir these ingredients together with a wooden spoon; put the mixture into a lined saucepan, place it over the fire, and stir until the substance is thick and soft. Put in a little salt, according to the age of the cheese, and a good sprinkling of pepper; and serve the fondue on a very hot silver or metal plate. Do not allow the fondue to remain on the fire after the mixture is set, as, if it boils, it will be entirely spoiled. Brillat-Savarin recommends that some choice Burgundy should be handed round with this dish. We have given this recipe exactly as he recommends it to be made; but we have tried it with good Cheshire cheese, and found it answer remarkably well.

Time – About 4 minutes to set the mixture.

Average cost for 4 persons, 10*d*.

Sufficient – Allow 1 egg, with the other ingredients in proportion, for one person. *Seasonable* – at any time.

EGGS À LA MÂITRE D'HÔTEL

Ingredients – ¼ lb. of fresh butter, 1 tablespoonful of flour, ½ pint of milk, pepper and salt to taste, 1 tablespoonful of minced parsley, the juice of ½ lemon, 6 eggs.

Mode – Put the flour and half the butter into a stew-pan; stir them over the fire until the mixture thickens; pour in the milk, which should be boiling; add a seasoning of pepper and salt, and simmer the whole for 5 minutes.

Put the remainder of the butter into the sauce, and add the minced parsley; then boil the eggs hard, strip off the shells, cut the eggs into quarters, and put them on a dish. Bring the sauce to the boiling-point, add the lemon-juice, pour over the eggs, and serve.
Time – 5 minutes to boil the sauce; the eggs, 10 to 15 minutes.
Average cost – 1s. *Seasonable* – at any time.
Sufficient for 4 or 5 persons.

Veneration for Eggs

Many of the most learned philosophers held eggs in a kind of respect, approaching to veneration, because they saw in them the emblem of the world and the four elements. The shell, they said, represented the earth; the white, water; the yolk, fire; and air was found under the shell at one end of the egg.

Recipes for Cakes

CHRISTMAS CAKE

Ingredients – 5 teacupfuls of flour, 1 teacupful of melted butter, 1 teacupful of cream, 1 teacupful of treacle, 1 teacupful of moist sugar, 2 eggs, ½ oz. of powdered ginger, ½ lb. of raisins, 1 teaspoonful of carbonate of soda, 1 tablespoonful of vinegar.

Mode – Make the butter sufficiently warm to melt it, but do not allow it to oil; put the flour into a basin; add to it the sugar, ginger, and raisins, which should be stoned and cut into small pieces. When these dry ingredients are thoroughly mixed, stir in the butter, cream, treacle, and well-whisked eggs, and beat the mixture for a few minutes. Dissolve the soda in the vinegar, add it to the dough, and be particular that these latter ingredients are well incorporated with the others; put the cake into a buttered mould or tin, place it in a moderate oven immediately, and bake it from 1¾ to 2¼ hours.

Time – 1¾ to 2¼ hours.

Average cost – 1*s*. 6*d*.

COMMON CAKE

Suitable for sending to children at school

Ingredients – 2 lb. of flour, 4 oz. of butter or clarified dripping, ½ oz. of caraway seeds, ¼ oz. of allspice, ½ lb. of pounded sugar, 1 lb. of currants, 1 pint of milk, 3 tablespoonfuls of fresh yeast.
Mode – Rub the butter lightly into the flour; add all the dry ingredients, and mix these well together. Make the milk warm, but not hot; stir in the yeast, and with this liquid make the whole into a light dough; knead it well, and line the cake-tins with strips of buttered paper; this paper should be about 6 inches higher than the top of the tin. Put in the dough; stand it in a warm place to rise for more than an hour; then bake the cakes in a well-heated oven. If this quantity be divided in two, they will take from 1½ to 2 hours' baking.
Time – 1¾ to 2¼ hours. *Average cost* – 1s. 9*d.*
Sufficient to make 2 moderate-sized cakes.

THICK GINGERBREAD

Ingredients – 1 lb. of treacle, ¼ lb. of butter, ¼ lb. of coarse brown sugar, 1½ lb. of flour, 1 oz. of ginger, ½ oz. of ground allspice, 1 teaspoonful of carbonate of soda, ¼ pint of warm milk, 3 eggs.
Mode – Put the flour into a basin, with the sugar, ginger, and allspice; mix these together; warm the butter, and add it, with the treacle, to the other ingredients. Stir well; make the milk just warm, dissolve the carbonate of

soda in it, and mix the whole into a nice smooth dough with the eggs, which should be previously well whisked; pour the mixture into a buttered tin, and bake it from ¾ to 1 hour, or longer, should the gingerbread be very thick. Just before it is done, brush the top over with the yolk of an egg beaten up with a little milk, and put it back in the oven to finish baking.

Time – ¾ to 1 hour.
Average cost – 1*s*. per square.
Seasonable – at any time.

Recipes for Beverages

TEA AND COFFEE

It is true, says Liebig, that thousands have lived without a knowledge of tea and coffee; and daily experience teaches us that, under certain circumstances, they may be dispensed with without disadvantage to the merely animal functions; but it is an error, certainly, to conclude from this that they may be altogether dispensed with in reference to their effects; and it is a question whether, if we had no tea and no coffee, the popular instinct would not seek for and discover the means of replacing them. Science, which accuses us of so much in these respects, will have, in the first place, to ascertain whether it depends on sensual and sinful inclinations merely, that every people of the globe have appropriated some such means of acting on the nervous life, from the shore of the Pacific, where the Indian retires from life for days in order to enjoy the bliss of intoxication with koko, to the Arctic regions, where Kamtschatdales and Koriakes prepare an intoxicating beverage from a poisonous mushroom. We think it, on the contrary, highly probable, not to say certain, that the instinct of man, feeling certain blanks, certain wants of the intensified life of our times, which cannot be satisfied or filled up by mere quantity, has discovered in these products of vegetable life the true means of giving to his food the desired and necessary quality.

TO ROAST COFFEE

A French Recipe

It being an acknowledged fact that French coffee is decidedly superior to that made in England, and as the roasting of the berry is of great importance to the flavour of the preparation, it will be useful and interesting to know how they manage these things in France. In Paris, there are two houses justly celebrated for the flavour of their coffee – La Maison Corcellet and La Maison Royer de Chartres; and to obtain this flavour, before roasting they add to every 3 lb. of coffee a piece of butter the size of a nut, and a dessertspoonful of powdered sugar: it is then roasted in the usual manner. The addition of the butter and sugar develops the flavour and aroma of the berry; but it must be borne in mind, that the quality of the butter must be of the very best description.

TO MAKE TEA

There is very little art in making good tea; if the water is boiling, and there is no sparing of the fragrant leaf, the beverage will almost invariably be good. The old-fashioned plan of allowing a teaspoonful to each person, and one over, is still practised. Warm the teapot with boiling water; let it remain for two or three minutes for the vessel to become thoroughly hot, then pour it away. Put in the tea, pour in from ½ to ¾ pint of boiling water, close the lid, and let it stand for the tea to draw from 5 to 10 minutes; then fill up the pot with water. The tea will be quite spoiled unless made with water that is actually 'boiling', as the leaves will not open, and the flavour not be extracted from them; the beverage will consequently be colourless and tasteless – in fact, nothing but tepid water. Where there is a very large party to make tea for, it is a good plan to have two teapots instead of putting a large quantity of tea into one pot; the tea, besides, will go farther. When the infusion has been once completed, the addition of fresh tea adds very little to the strength; so, when more is required, have the pot emptied of the old leaves, scalded, and fresh tea made in the usual manner. Economists say that a few grains of carbonate of soda, added before the boiling water is poured on the tea, assist to draw out the goodness: if the water is very hard, perhaps it is a good plan, as the soda softens it; but care must be taken to use this ingredient sparingly, as it is liable to give the tea a soapy taste if added in too large a quantity. For mixed tea, the usual proportion is four spoonfuls of black to one of green; more of the latter when the flavour is very much liked; but strong green tea is highly pernicious, and should never be partaken of too freely.

Time – 2 minutes to warm the teapot, 5 to 10 minutes to draw the strength from the tea. *Sufficient* – Allow 1 teaspoonful to each person, and one over.

AN EXCELLENT SUBSTITUTE FOR MILK OR CREAM IN TEA AND COFFEE

Ingredients – Allow 1 new-laid egg to every large breakfast-cupful of tea or coffee.
Mode – Beat up the whole of the egg in a basin, put it into a cup (or a portion of it, if the cup be small), and pour over it the tea or coffee very hot. These should be added very gradually, and stirred all the time, to prevent the egg from curdling. In point of nourishment, both these beverages are much improved by this addition.
Sufficient – Allow 1 egg to every large breakfast-cupful of tea or coffee.

COWSLIP WINE

Ingredients – To every gallon of water allow 3 lb. of lump sugar, the rind of 2 lemons, the juice of 1, the rind and juice of 1 Seville orange, 1 gallon of cowslip pips. To every 4½ gallons of wine allow 1 bottle of brandy.
Mode – Boil the sugar and water together for ½ hour, carefully removing all the scum as it rises. Pour this boiling liquor on the orange and lemon-rinds, and the juice, which should be strained; when milk-warm, add the cowslip pips or flowers, picked from the stalks and seeds; and to 9 gallons of wine 3 tablespoonfuls of good fresh brewers' yeast. Let it ferment 3 or 4 days; then put all together in a cask with the brandy, and let it remain for 2 months, when bottle it off for use.
Time – To be boiled ½ hour; to ferment 3 or 4 days; to

remain in the cask 2 months. *Average cost* – exclusive of the cowslips, which may be picked in the fields, 2*s*. 9*d*. per gallon. *Seasonable* – Make this in April or May.

LEMONADE

Ingredients – The rind of 2 lemons, the juice of 3 large or 4 small ones, 1 lb. of loaf sugar, 1 quart of boiling water. *Mode* – Rub some of the sugar, in lumps, on 2 of the lemons until they have imbibed all the oil from them, and put it with the remainder of the sugar into a jug; add the lemon-juice (but no pips), and pour over the whole a quart of boiling water. When the sugar is dissolved, strain the lemonade through a fine sieve or piece of muslin, and, when cool, it will be ready for use. The lemonade will be much improved by having the white of an egg beaten up in it; a little sherry mixed with it, also, makes this beverage much nicer.
Average cost – 6*d*. per quart.

'There is a current opinion among women,' says Brillat-Savarin, 'which every year causes the death of many young women – that acids, especially vinegar, are preventives of obesity. Beyond all doubt, acids have the effect of destroying obesity; but they also destroy health and freshness. Lemonade is, of all acids, the most harmless; but few stomachs can resist it long. I knew, in 1776, at Dijon, a young lady of great beauty, to whom I was attached by bonds of friendship, great, almost as those of love. One day, when she had for some time gradually grown pale and thin (previously she had a slight *embonpoint*), she told me in confidence that as her young friends had ridiculed her for being fat, she had, to counteract the tendency, been in the habit every day of drinking a large glass of *vinaigre*. She died at eighteen years of age, from the effects of these potions.'

TO MAKE HOT PUNCH

Ingredients – ½ pint of rum, ½ pint of brandy, ¼ lb. of sugar, 1 large lemon, ½ teaspoonful of nutmeg, 1 pint of boiling water.

Mode – Rub the sugar over the lemon until it has absorbed all the yellow part of the skin, then put the sugar into a punchbowl; add the lemon-juice (free from pips), and mix these two ingredients well together. Pour over them the boiling water, stir well together, add the rum, brandy, and nutmeg; mix thoroughly, and the punch will be ready to serve. It is very important in making good punch that all the ingredients are thoroughly incorporated; and, to insure success, the processes of mixing must be diligently attended to.

Sufficient – Allow a quart for 4 persons; but this information must be taken *cum grano salis*; for the capacities of persons for this kind of beverage are generally supposed to vary considerably.

Recipes for Invalid Cookery

BARLEY GRUEL

Ingredients – 2 oz. of Scotch or pearl barley, ½ pint of port wine, the rind of 1 lemon, 1 quart and ½ pint of water, sugar to taste.
Mode – After well washing the barley, boil it in ½ pint of water for ¼ hour, then pour this water away; put to the barley the quart of fresh boiling water, and let it boil until the liquid is reduced to half; then strain it off. Add the wine, sugar, and lemon-peel; simmer for 5 minutes, and put it away in a clean jug. It can be warmed from time to time, as required.
Time – To be boiled until reduced to half. *Average cost* – 1*s*. 6*d*.
Sufficient with the wine to make 1½ pint of gruel.

EEL BROTH

Ingredients – ½ lb. of eels, a small bunch of sweet herbs, including parsley; ½ onion, 10 peppercorns, 3 pints of water, 2 cloves, salt and pepper to taste.
Mode – After having cleaned and skinned the eel, cut it into small pieces, and put it into a stewpan, with the other ingredients; simmer gently until the liquid is reduced nearly half, carefully removing the scum as it

rises. Strain it through a hair sieve; put it by in a cool place, and, when wanted, take off all the fat from the top, warm up as much as is required, and serve with sippets of toasted bread. This is a very nutritious broth, and easy of digestion.
Time – To be simmered until the liquor is reduced to half.
Average cost – 6*d*.
Sufficient to make 1½ pint of broth.
Seasonable – from June to March.

INVALID'S JELLY

Ingredients – 12 shanks of mutton, 3 quarts of water, a bunch of sweet herbs, pepper and salt to taste, 3 blades of mace, 1 onion, 1 lb. of lean beef, a crust of bread toasted brown.
Mode – Soak the shanks in plenty of water for some hours, and scrub them well; put them, with the beef and other ingredients, into a saucepan with the water, and let them simmer very gently for 5 hours. Strain the broth, and, when cold, take off all the fat. It may be eaten either warmed up or cold as a jelly.
Time – 5 hours. *Average cost* – 1*s*. Sufficient to make from 1½ to 2 pints of jelly. *Seasonable* – at any time.

TO MAKE MUTTON BROTH

Ingredients – 1 lb. of the scrag end of the neck of mutton, 1 onion, a bunch of sweet herbs, ½ turnip, 3 pints of water, pepper and salt to taste.

Mode – Put the mutton into a stewpan; pour over the water cold and add the other ingredients. When it boils, skim it very carefully, cover the pan closely, and let it simmer very gently for an hour; strain it, let it cool, take off all the fat from the surface, and warm up as much as may be required, adding, if the patient be allowed to take it, a teaspoonful of minced parsley which has been previously scalded. Pearl barley or rice are very nice additions to mutton broth, and should be boiled as long as the other ingredients. When either of these is added, the broth must not be strained, but merely thoroughly skimmed. Plain mutton broth without seasoning is made by merely boiling the mutton, water, and salt together, straining it, letting the broth cool, skimming all the fat off, and warming up as much as is required. This preparation would be very tasteless and insipid, but likely to agree with very delicate stomachs, whereas the least addition of other ingredients would have the contrary effect.

Time – 1 hour. *Average cost – 7d.*

Sufficient to make from 1½ to 2 pints of broth.

Seasonable – at any time.

Note – Veal broth may be made in the same manner; the knuckle of a leg or shoulder is the part usually used for this purpose. It is very good with the addition of the inferior joints of a fowl, or a few shank-bones.

A LITTLE DINNER BEFORE THE PLAY

Agnes Jekyll

WHETHER EXTOLLING THE MERITS of a cheerful breakfast tray, conjuring up a winter picnic of figs and mulled wine, sharing delicious Tuscan recipes, or suggesting a last-minute pre-theatre dinner, the sparkling writings of the society hostess and philanthropist Agnes Jekyll describe food for every imaginable occasion and mood.

Originally published in *The Times* in the early 1920s, these divinely witty and brilliantly observed pieces are still loved today for their warmth and friendly advice and, with their emphasis on fresh, simple, stylish dishes, were years ahead of their time.

'Beautifully written, sparkling, witty and knowing, an absolute delight to read'

INDIA KNIGHT

A DISSERTATION UPON ROAST PIG & OTHER ESSAYS

Charles Lamb

A RAPTUROUS APPRECIATION of pork crackling, a touching description of hungry London chimney sweeps, a discussion of the strange pleasure of eating pineapple and a meditation on the delights of Christmas feasting are just some of the subjects of these personal, playful writings from early nineteenth-century essayist Charles Lamb.

Exploring the joys of food and also our complicated social relationship with it, these essays are by turns sensuous, mischievous, lyrical and self-mocking. Filled with a sense of hunger, they are some of the most fascinating and nuanced works ever written about eating, drinking and appetite.

'The Georgian essayist, tender and puckish, with a weakness for oddity and alcohol, is one of the great chroniclers of London'

OBSERVER

BUFFALO CAKE AND INDIAN PUDDING

Dr A. W. Chase

TRAVELLING PHYSICIAN, SALESMAN, author and self-made man, Dr Chase dispensed remedies all over America during the late nineteenth century, collecting recipes and domestic tips from the people he met along the way. His self-published books became celebrated US bestsellers and were the household bibles of their day.

Containing recipes for American-style treats, such as Boston cream cakes, Kentucky corn dodgers and pumpkin pie, as well as genial advice on baking bread and testing whether a cake is cooked, this is a treasure trove of culinary wisdom from the homesteads of a still rural, pioneering United States.

EXCITING FOOD FOR SOUTHERN TYPES

Pellegrino Artusi

PELLEGRINO ARTUSI is the original icon of Italian cookery, whose legendary 1891 book *Science in the Kitchen and the Art of Eating Well* defined its national cuisine and is still a bestseller today.

He was also a passionate gastronome, renowned host and brilliant raconteur, who filled his books with tasty recipes and rumbustious anecdotes. From an unfortunate incident regarding minestrone in Livorno and a proud defence of the humble meat loaf, to digressions on the unusual history of ice-cream, the side-effects of cabbage and the Florentines' weak constitutions, these writings brim with gossip, good cheer and an inexhaustible zest for life.

'The fountainhead of modern Italian cookery'
GASTRONOMICA

THE JOYS OF EXCESS

Samuel Pepys

AS WELL AS BEING THE MOST celebrated diarist of all time, Samuel Pepys was also a hearty drinker, eater and connoisseur of epicurean delights, who indulged in every pleasure seventeenth-century London had to offer.

Whether he is feasting on barrels of oysters, braces of carps, larks' tongues and copious amounts of wine, merrymaking in taverns until the early hours, attending formal dinners with lords and ladies or entertaining guests at home with his young wife, these irresistible selections from Pepys's diaries provide a frank, high-spirited and vivid picture of the joys of over-indulgence – and the side-effects afterwards.

'Vigorous, precise, enchanting . . . the most ordinary and the most extraordinary writer you will ever meet'

CLAIRE TOMALIN

FROM ABSINTHE TO ZEST

An Alphabet for Food Lovers

Alexandre Dumas

AS WELL AS BEING THE AUTHOR OF *The Three Musketeers*, Alexandre Dumas was also an enthusiastic gourmand and expert cook. His *Grand Dictionnaire de Cuisine*, published in 1873, is an encyclopaedic collection of ingredients, recipes and anecdotes, from Absinthe to Zest via cake, frogs' legs, oysters, roquefort and vanilla.

Included here are recipes for bamboo pickle and strawberry omelette, advice on cooking all manner of beast from bear to kangaroo – as well as delightful digressions into how a fig started a war and whether truffles really increase ardour – brought together in a witty and gloriously eccentric culinary compendium.

'From the great French novelist and obsessive gourmet. The cook book as literature'
NORMAN SPINRAD